THROUGH THE YELLOWSTONE PARK

D1738684

(*Frontispiece.*)

"TEMPTED TO FREEDOM."

For Cathy from Gordon,
One mild Westerner to another,
26 January 2000

THROUGH THE

YELLOWSTONE PARK

ON HORSEBACK

BY
GEORGE W. WINGATE

FOREWORD BY
GORDON B. DODDS

ILLUSTRATED

University of Idaho Press
Moscow, Idaho
1999

Originally published in 1886 by O. Judd Co., David W. Judd, Pres't.,
751 Broadway, New York.
Introduction by Gordon B. Dodds © 1999 by the
University of Idaho Press
Published by the University of Idaho Press,
Moscow, Idaho 83844-1107
Printed in the United States of America
All Rights Reserved

Idaho Yesterdays is a reprint series developed and published by the
Idaho State Historical Society and the University of Idaho Press.

Cover image: The Grand Canyon of the Yellowstone, 1893-1901; Thomas
Moran, 1928.7.1

National Museum of American Art, Smithsonian Institution, Washington,
D.C./Art Resource, N.Y.

Map of the Yellowstone National Park compiled from different official
explorations and our personal survey, 1882. Carl J. Hals and A. Rydstrom,
Civil Engineers. Courtesy University of Idaho Library, Moscow, Idaho.

03 02 01 00 99   5 4 3 2 1

Library of Congress Cataloging-in-Publication Data

Wingate, George Wood, 1840–1928.
    Through the Yellowstone Park on horseback / by George W.
 Wingate; foreword by Gordon B. Dodds.
        p.   cm. — (Idaho yesterdays)
    "Originally published in 1886 by O. Judd Co., David W.
 Judd. Pres't., New York"—T.p. verso.
    ISBN 0-89301-205-X (alk. paper)
        1. Yellowstone National Park—Description and travel.
    2. Wingate, George Wood, 1840–1928—Journeys—Yellowstone
    National Park. 3. Packhorse camping—Yellowstone National
    Park. 4. Yellowstone National Park—History.   I. Title.
    II. Series: Idaho yesterdays (Moscow, Idaho)
    F722.W76   1999
        917.87'520433—dc21   96-29682
                                                          CIP

CONTENTS.

———

Page.

ILLUSTRATIONS.

INTRODUCTION

BY GORDON B. DODDS

In July and August of 1885, George Wood Wingate, a wealthy and prominent New Yorker, his wife, and their seventeen-year-old daughter took a horseback trip through Yellowstone National Park. It gave them one of the greatest experiences of their lives, and it inspired him to write this book. No one has ever written a better travel account of the Park than George Wingate, and few have produced better books about it in any genre. Humane, detailed, and accurate, *Through the Yellowstone Park on Horseback* is a treat for historians, scientists, and lovers of the national parks.

The author of this travelogue was a successful soldier, lawyer, and politician. Born in New York City on July 1, 1840, he graduated from its public schools and had some education at the Free Academy—now the City College of New York. When the Civil War broke out he joined the Twenty-second Regiment of the New York State National Guard as a private, rising to the rank of captain. He served with his unit at Baltimore, at Harper's Ferry, and during Lee's invasion of Pennsylvania that culminated in the Battle of Gettysburg. After the war he obtained the rank of brigadier general in his role as Inspector General of the National Guard from 1874 to 1876.

Wingate began the study of law in an attorney's office at the age of thirteen and was admitted to the bar in 1861. He began practice after the war with the firm of Lord, Day & Lord in New York City, then founded a firm with William C. Whitney in 1866 and another with Henry J. Cullen in 1873. He remained connected with this last firm until his death in 1928. He was an investor in the Long Island Railroad, of which he was also assistant general counsel, and in the elevated railroad system of Brooklyn. Wingate entered the political realm as one of the prominent business and professional supporters (the Swallowtails) of Tammany Hall, New York City's Democratic political machine. He represented the organization in political cases and was a member of its governing council (the Sachems) in the 1870s; he also represented in the courts two of Tammany's political bosses, Richard Croker and John Kelly.

Always interested in outdoor recreation, public education, and athletic and military training, Wingate pursued those interests in a variety of ways. He was a member of the New York City Board of Education from 1901 to 1918 and founded the Public Schools Athletic League in order to provide healthy recreational activities for city children. In his role as an official of the National Guard, he introduced regular rifle practice as a part of its training. But the National Rifle Association was his most enduring legacy. William Conant Church and George W. Wingate, both Civil War officers who had been dismayed at the lack of marksmanship displayed in the Union Army, obtained a charter for the NRA in New York State on November 17, 1871. He was its first secretary and later its president for twenty-five years.

Wingate was a prolific author, and his writing reflects his interests. In addition to the present volume, he published pamphlets on the history of the Twenty-second Regiment, instructions for rifle practice, pleas for instruction in riflery and military training in the public schools, and the very popular *Manual for Rifle Practice*, which went through seven printings between 1872 and 1880. In addition he wrote many articles for the *Journal of the Military Service Institute* and the *Army and Navy Journal*—both edited by William C. Church.

In June of 1885 this quintessential city man went west. His purpose was to take his wife, Susan, and elder daughter, May, to Yellowstone Park in the hope that the journey would restore the young woman to health. Although the park was thirteen years old when they set out, Wingate declared that "if I had been going to Africa instead of the Yellowstone, I could scarcely have had more trouble in obtaining reliable information in regard to the journey." The book he wrote in the year following the family's expedition would provide for others the information that he had lacked. It is a colorful and accurate account of the seasonal and permanent occupants, flora and fauna, and geysers and canyons of the area that people then called "Wonderland." Wingate had a knack for capturing the telling detail of a grand region without descent into purple prose or exaggeration. He was appreciative, humorous, and unafraid to admit his own "greenhorn's" mistakes.

Yellowstone, the world's first national park, was created by an act of Congress in 1872. By that time many people had passed through its confines. The area comprising the park had been inhabited by Native American peoples for hundreds of years. The first white men who entered the area are not known by name but surely were from among the ranks of the beaver trappers. It is possible that the first of these to see the area that became Yellowstone Park was John Colter, a fur hunter, teller of tales, and a member of the Lewis and Clark expedition, but no one knows for sure if he deserves the honor. Certainly other mountain men, such as the famed Jim Bridger, did cross the region that later became the park when seeking beaver and when making their way to the great annual rendezvous of trappers and their suppliers in the sheltered mountain parks of the Rockies in the 1820s and 1830s. A party of miners visited a portion of the future park in 1863, and more followed soon thereafter. Farmers, stockmen, and town dwellers in the surrounding region also learned about the unusual landscape and its unique natural features.

In 1869 three relatively obscure residents of Montana Territory, Charles W. Cook, David E. Folsom, and William Peterson, made the first systematic exploration of the Yellowstone region. Although their journey was not widely reported, it piqued the interest of important people who wanted to see the wonders for themselves. In August and September of 1870 a group of Montanans traversed a part of what became the park and were led by General Henry D. Washburn, a veteran of the Civil War who was then Surveyor General of Montana Territory. The group's other prominent members included Cornelius Hedges, soon to be Montana's territorial Superintendent of Public Instruction, and Nathaniel P. Langford, who two years later would become the park's first (and unpaid) superintendent. Langford had come to Montana Territory in 1862 with a military expedition and stayed to become both a noted vigilante and a territorial official.

The Washburn expedition's report was published and received a good deal of attention, mainly because one of its members was lost for thirty-seven days. A more important reaction came from the Northern Pacific railroad, whose tracks were approaching the Yellowstone country. The railroad's executives saw the region as a potential source of tourist revenue, and they hired Langford to publicize the area in the East. Langford's speeches interested Ferdinand V. Hayden of the United States Geological and Geographical Survey of the Territories. Hayden persuaded Congress to give him the authority to investigate Yellowstone scientifically through a survey that he conducted in 1871. Hayden's report was well documented, not only in his own words but through illustrations furnished by photographer William Henry Jackson and landscape painter Thomas Moran.

These travelers' accounts, whether amateur, professional, scientific, literary, or artistic, helped create the Yellowstone Park. The Park's origins are complex. The natural wonders of canyons, geysers, and hot springs were innately interesting to all who saw them. The federal government had established a kind of precedent by setting aside part of the Yosemite region in California in 1864 as a federal reserve—but not a park. Some Americans may have regarded the Yellowstone region's majestic and unique natural beauty as a defining theme of the nation, making up for the lack of historical associations, monuments, and cultural achievements that were regarded as distinguishing Europe and Great Britain. And, regardless of the motives of its proponents, those who wanted a park were able to carry out the innovative plan because the land was looked upon as "worthless" for economic pursuits such as agriculture, lumbering, mining, and ranching.

By the time the Wingates made their journey, the park had already been the site of administrative struggles, lack of funding and facilities, failed concessions, and conflict between tourists and Nez Perce Indians trying to flee to Canada during the Nez Perce War of 1877. In 1886, the U.S. Army would take over management of the park from the Department of the Interior; with the establishment of the National Park Service in 1918, management would return to civilian hands. But even in its first years, Yellowstone attracted a significant number of visitors, many of them prominent individuals (including President Chester A. Arthur, who made his well-publicized trip in 1883). Thus the Wingate party was participating in a growing pilgrimage to the natural wonders of the West.

As befitted their station in life, the Wingates traveled in comfort. They took the train from New York to Chicago, changed again in St. Paul, and descended from the Northern Pacific train at Bozeman. Although they could have taken a branch line closer to the park entrance, they chose Bozeman because of its proximity to Fort Ellis, where they hoped to persuade some of the Army officers stationed there and their families to accompany them.

The party outfitted itself at Bozeman. Wingate hired three men: a guide, Jim Fisher; his partner; and a cook. These three, Wingate wrote, "were the best type of Western frontiersmen, quiet, self-respecting, obliging, and always respectful." Each traveler had a saddle horse, and four other horses pulled a large wagon. Into this vehicle went every conceivable article, supplies such as goggles, buffalo robes, and books; a wall tent in which everyone but the guides and cook slept; food and drink, including sixty pounds of bacon, six dozen eggs, three cans of tongue, two cases of beer, and six quarts of whiskey. Given Wingate's interest in hunting and marksmanship, it is not surprising that the wagon also carried arms and ammunition—or that he devoted a good many words to such topics.

What distinguished Wingate's party from those of most wealthy tourists—and why he chose his book's title—was that the group traveled on horseback, rather than being conveyed by stagecoach or wagon. Another distinctive factor of Wingate's party was that they slept in a tent rather than in hotels; part of the reason for this choice may have been the assortment of flimsy wooden structures and tents that most hotels in the park were at the time—not only ill constructed but often totally lacking in privacy. President Arthur's group had camped out as well, to the dismay of some concessionaires. Certainly both transportation and housing added to the trip's success.

Once equipped, the party set out from Fort Ellis traveling east along the route of the Northern Pacific and then, proceeding southeast and then south, approximately along the track of contemporary Trail Creek Road until they reached the junction of Eight Mile Creek and the Yellowstone River. Following the course of the Yellowstone, they continued south past the little town of Gardiner to the park headquarters at Mammoth Springs (now Mammoth Hot Springs). There they were joined by the post surgeon from Fort Ellis, his wife, and their young son. The next leg of the journey took them to the Norris Basin and on to Gibbon Cañon and Falls and to the great geysers of the Upper Geyser Basin. After viewing this unique spectacle and after a memorable stay in the Grand Cañon of the Yellowstone, the party traced its way back toward Bozeman via the northwest portion of the park, over the Continental Divide at Targhee Pass, and up the Madison Valley. All in all, the six visitors and their crew spent twenty-six days traveling 460 miles, most of them within the park boundaries.

Wingate's narrative includes descriptions of the natural wonders, laced with rich metaphors, that convey the party's awe. The author was a good storyteller, capturing the unusual, quirky, and funny occurrences that the party experienced—many of which arose from the unfamiliar landscape and creatures. His observant eye was caught as much by the people of Yellowstone as by the wonders of the natural environment. In the park his party encountered a diverse group of men and women—some familiar, some strange, some expected, some unexpected. All were described with sympathy rather than caricature, and Wingate took pains to put them in the context of western rather than eastern experience.

Wingate designed *Through the Yellowstone Park on Horseback* to be helpful as well as entertaining. He considered his audience to include those visitors—not as hardy as his family—who would travel by stage rather than horseback. For them, he described the quality of the roads; the rates at the hotels, their opening and closing dates, and their furnishings; and the travel times on the stagecoaches between them. For readers who would camp as his party did, he included long lists of what to take. For both groups—and for the armchair traveler—he provided chapters on flora and fauna of the park, elevations of its various regions, and suggested itineraries and timetables. Further, Wingate's shrewd eye and discerning pen gave his readers pictures of landscape and places along his route before and after they reached the park: the cities of St. Paul and Minneapolis; the modulated voices and distinctive attire of the western male; the bonanza farms of the Great Plains; the drabness of the little towns; the culture of the cattle industry; the Native Americans; the weird landscape of the Badlands; the military routine at Fort Ellis; and a female elected official in Montana Territory.

Filled with their impressions of nature, colorful adventures, and unforgettable characters, the Wingate family returned to New York City in August. Their expedition had been a complete success. The daughter's health was restored, the mother enjoyed almost every minute (and gained twelve pounds), and the father produced this jewel of a travel book. Readers should be grateful for the eastern physicians who did not cure May Wingate: if they had, there would have been no horseback journey through the park, no adventures amidst its wonders, and no book to describe them so graphically.

To put their trip in perspective, on their way home the Wingates stopped at Niagara Falls, supposedly the nation's greatest natural feature, "to show it to my daughter and a niece who accompanied us home, but after the scenery we had witnessed, Niagara looked flat and tired." No American traveler could pay a finer tribute to Yellowstone.

THROUGH THE

YELLOWSTONE PARK

ON HORSEBACK.

CHAPTER I.

THE YELLOWSTONE PARK, AND HOW TO REACH IT.

In June, 1885, I decided to undertake a trip through the Rocky Mountains, with my wife and eldest daughter, a young lady of seventeen. The latter had been quite ill during the preceding winter from an affection of the lungs, and I was advised that exercise and open air life at a high altitude would remove all traces of her disease, a result which I am glad to say was fully accomplished by the trip.

If I had been going to Africa instead of to the Yellowstone, I could scarcely have had more trouble in obtaining reliable information in regard to the journey; and while I have undertaken, for the benefit of friends, to write such an account of it as my time will permit, I do so with the hope that it may perchance relieve others contemplating such an excursion from some of the difficulties that I experienced, in trying to learn what was to be done and what avoided.

(9)

I was told by the best authority " that the flies would be insupportable during July." " It would be too hot." " It would be too cold."—" The roads would be abominable."—" I would find no game."—" The fish would not take a fly," and many similar statements.

With these warnings in our ears, it required some courage to undertake the trip ; the more so as I proposed to make it on horseback, and as neither my wife nor daughter were accustomed to the saddle. But we decided to go, and go we did ; and now that we are safely back, better and stronger than we have been for years, we are united in the opinion that it has been the most enjoyable trip of our lives. In twenty-six days, counting from the time we left the railroad, we rode upwards of four hundred and sixty miles, over prairies and mountains, through rocky cañons and along frowning precipices, enjoying the most magnificent scenery that the world affords, until we were all as brown as Indians and able to spend eight hours a day in the saddle without excessive fatigue, and this without accident or serious risk.

The Yellowstone Park is a reservation which was withdrawn by the United States Congress in 1872 from settlement, and devoted to the purposes of a National Park "for the pleasure and enjoyment of the people." It is under the control of the Secretary of the Interior, who is represented by a Superintendent, who resides at the Mammoth Springs, and who has under him a number of men who protect the game, prevent vandalism by tourists (no easy task), and the destruction of the timber by fire. There is also a corps of laborers under army engineers constantly at work building roads and bridges, and improving the means of communication. A detachment from the United States Geological Survey has also been stationed in the Park since its establishment.

The hotels in the Park were constructed by the Yellowstone Park Company (organized by Mr. Rufus Hatch) under a contract with the Secretary of the Interior, and it provides a stage line and other matters required for the accommodation of tourists.

The National Park lies mainly in the north-western part of Wyoming, although a narrow strip of southern Montana and south-eastern Idaho is also included, and extends from about 110° west longitude to a few miles west of the meridan of 111°, and is between 44° and 45° north latitude. To call this region a park, is to convey a false impression, as it is fifty-five miles long by sixty-five wide, contains 3,575 square miles, and is larger than Rhode Island and Delaware combined, and is two-thirds as large as Connecticut.

Its altitude is very great. The lowest valleys are 6,000 feet above the sea, and several are 1,000 to 2,000 feet higher. The mountains which border on these valleys attain a hight of from 10,000 to 12,000 feet. The Park is of volcanic origin, and therefore devoid of minerals. As the nights are seldom free from frost, farming is an impossibility, although flowers grow luxuriantly. But though of no mercantile value, the Park is full of natural wonders which eminently fit it for the purposes for which it has been so wisely set apart. Here are found the greatest geysers known, beside which those of Iceland sink into insignificance ; here are hot springs of every imaginable color, interspersed with springs of mud, sulphur, iron, alum, and of every possible chemical known to the vagaries of nature. Deep cañons, snow-clad mountains, mighty cataracts, beautiful lakes, are here found combined in a manner that exists nowhere else.

The various attractions of the Park are considerable distances apart, the Springs being twenty-one miles from the Lower Geysers, which in turn are twenty-six miles from the Great Geysers, and the latter thirty miles from the Great Cañon. A large force has been at work under army engineers for a long while, improving the means of access and travel ; and so many improvements have been made, particularly during the last year, that whatever may have been the case heretofore, the Park is now traversed by the best roads I have ever seen in a mountain country.   In fact, with the exception of a few heavy grades, one short space of sandy road, a part of the road to the Great Cañon, and the stretch from the Firehole River to the Madison Basin, the main roads within the Park can be called good.   A light buggy, drawn by a spirited horse, was driven with us all through it without difficulty.

The Park is much easier of access than is generally supposed.   The Northern Pacific Rail Road operates a branch from its main line at Livingston to Cinnabar, which connects by stages with the hotel at Mammoth Springs, a distance of only six miles, and which is the best method of approach.

While there are several picturesque places which are only accessible on horseback, the main points of interest in the Park are reached by comfortable covered stages which start daily from this hotel, and which are used by the great majority of visitors, whose time is usually limited, or who do not care to endure the fatigue of riding. There is not the least necessity for a visitor who proposes to adopt this method of traveling, to provide any camping outfit or stock of provisions ; or, in fact, making any more preparation than would be the case in going to the White Mountains.   He will find at each stopping place a fair hotel, where he can remain as long as he pleases, provided he gives notice of his intention to stop over. Our party did not stop at any of these hotels, and I cannot therefore say anything in regard to them from personal experience.   I was informed by those of my friends who did stop there, that the fare was good, (except at the Fire Hole Hotel, where they were suffering from a bad Chinese cook), but that with the exception of the large hotel at the Mammoth Springs, which is fitted up and managed in city fashion, the sleeping accommodations in the others were primitive. The one at the Cañon was merely a series of large tents.

My friends also told me that the stage drivers were skillful, seeming to know every stump and stone on the road. A few were talkative, and would of themselves point out all the objects of interest. The majority were reticent, but when asked, could and did afford a good deal of information. All travelers know, however, that information received from professional stage-drivers by strangers is to be accepted with caution. One of the drivers gave a friend of mine a vast amount of information as to the habits and wonders of the West, describing in particular a celebrated team he once had of eighteen mules that were so well trained that when he whistled, the whole eighteen would rush into their respective places, in front of his wagon, and stand there so that he had nothing to do but to drop the harness on them !

My friend happened to be conversant with the habits of that gentle animal, the mule, and was therefore able to justly estimate the probabilities of the story. He did not, however, cast any doubt upon the narrative, but having heard that the driver had never been over the road to the Great Cañon, gave him a thrilling account of the steepness of the descent from the top of the Divide, mentioning, as an instance, that the angle was so great in coming down that he and his driver stood on the dashboard all the way. On hearing this, the driver gave him a queer look and said nothing more about his mules.

Even those who make the tour of the Park in stages are not obliged to ride in them exclusively. If they desire to make any part of the trip on horseback, or to visit any of the objects of interest which are off the stage routes they can procure at the different hotels, horses and guides at a cost of $2.00 a day for the former, and $4.00 for the latter.

Neither does a trip through the Park involve the great expense that is generally supposed. Of course, if one goes with a party and an "outfit" (to use the Western term) of men and horses, the cost is considerable ; but a tour made in the stages is decidedly cheap when compared with the ordinary expense of a summer excursion of any length. The Northern Pacific Railroad sells excursion tickets from St. Paul through the Park by way of its Livingston branch, and return for $120, including Pullman sleeper, meals on dining cars, hotel accommodation and stages, and allowing a stay of five days in the Park.

To see the points of interest thoroughly, and particularly the Great Geysers, as well as to lessen the fatigue of continuous staging, three days more should be added, one to be spent at the Mammoth Springs and two at the Great Geysers. This will involve a further expense of four to five dollars a day. It will also be wise to ride out to the East and Middle Falls of the Gardner, which will require a guide and horse for one day each. On the whole, the trip from St. Paul can be well done for $150, and in twelve days, (the schedule time is nine days). One of my friends who went through by stage, and did not hire any horses, but did stay two days over the schedule time, said that it cost him for everything, less than twenty dollars over the price of his excursion ticket. From New York it will cost about $200 to $250 for each person, and take a little less than three weeks. It will be found wise for those coming from the latter city to reduce the fatigue of such a long railroad journey by stopping over a day or two each way, either at St. Paul or Minneapolis, and perhaps at Chicago.

The Park hotels are open from June 15, to October ; but the best time to make the visit is during the months of July, August and September. The first two of these months are preferable ; as the altitude of the Park, particularly at the Great Cañon, is so great that snow may be expected in September. Everybody told us that we were making a great mistake in going in July, as the mosquitoes would then be frightful. I can only say that we saw very few, and no more in July than in August.

By going early in the season, not only is the crowd avoided, but the grazing is much better. Towards the last of the season the grass near the best camping grounds is nearly all consumed, and those who travel with their own outfit will need to carry grain for their animals. On the other hand, the later the season, the better the hunting outside the Park.

The visitor should by all means enter the Park by way of the Mammoth Springs. By doing this, the smaller geysers are seen first and the interest is kept excited ; while after seeing the Great Geysers, the others appear tame.

The route by the Northern Pacific, *via* Livingston, is the only one that should be taken. That by way of the Utah Northern involves a stage ride of one hundred and fourteen miles over a monotonous country, and brings the tourist in at the wrong part of the Park. The only train arrives and leaves Beaver Cañon at 1 A. M., and I was told that the accommodations there were wretched.

While traveling by the regular stages is the cheapest and shortest method and involves the least fatigue, all our party decidedly preferred the greater independence of having our own " outfit," and thought, and still think, that the scenery could be much better appreciated from the saddle than from a covered stage.

CHAPTER II.

THE RAILROAD JOURNEY.

The nine hundred and seventy-seven miles which lie between New York and Chicago, and the latter city itself, are too familiar to need comment. But upon entering Minnesota the alternation between the fertile prairies, with their scattered rows and clumps of timber, and the limestone crags which surmount the bluffs which overhang the valleys, at once attracted our attention, and impressed us with the beauties and fertility of that State.

We arrived at St. Paul on July 5th, 1885. This city and its neighboring, and to us more beautiful rival, Minneapolis had, of course, to be explored ; the charming falls of Minnehaha seen, and the great Washburn Mill, which turns out six thousand and two hundred barrels of flour a day, visited. In addition we had to see the old frontier, but now modernized post of Fort Snelling, and to pay our respects to General Terry, one of the many officers of our army, in whom the whole country feels a just pride ; so that it was not until July 8th, that we found ourselves on the cars of the Northern Pacific, *en route* for the Great West.

Those who are not familiar with American travel will be surprised to learn that although St. Paul is nearly one thousand and four hundred miles west from New York, there was little, if anything to be seen before reaching it, and nothing in the city itself to indicate that we were "out West." The most noticeable change being, that first the Chicago papers displaced those of the New York, and were in turn displaced by those of St. Paul. The people dressed, acted and talked as they do at the East. The hotels were as good—in fact the "Ryan" at St. Paul, and the "West" at Minneapolis were in our judgment superior to any hotels in New York. The two cities are but some ten miles apart, and communication is easy and frequent, yet the jealousy between them is extreme. If any business man wants to sell goods in either city it behooves him not to put up at the grand hotel of the other. In fact it is a standard joke that the blizzards which sweep down from the Northwest, have their origin in the excessive coolness which exists between St. Paul and Minneapolis. Even in the country, except for the broad prairies, and the limitation of timber to a strip along the roads and to the clumps around the houses (which have been cultivated as screens from the wind) and the limestone bluffs which overhang the valleys, one might well imagine himself still in the State of New York.

From St. Paul onward the indications that we were "out West" became greater. The broad-brimmed felt hat with a leather strap for a band, without which no self-respecting cattleman or cowboy permits himself to be seen, becomes more frequent. "Cayuse" ponies, with Mexican saddles and bridles were observed at the various stations, and finally we met the full-blown " cowboy " white-hatted, big-spurred, his legs encased in leather " chapareros " or overalls, loping over the prairie on a wiry pony, and swinging his lariat at every jump of the latter in the orthodox manner, as he rounded up his cattle. Appearances were sometimes deceptive on this point. As the train stopped at one station a horseman galloped up with the most orthodox equipment, whirling his noosed lariat over his head and bringing it down on his horse's flanks at every stride. On inquiry as to who that cowboy was? the answer was : " Oh, that is not a cowboy ; that is the village dentist ! " Of revolvers there was a great lack. I can only recollect seeing three during our whole trip. Neither did we see but two drunken men, and those were inoffensive. In over a month I heard decidedly less swearing than would be the case in one evening in a country store in the East, and witnessed not a single quarrel or even loud words. In fact, one of the things in Dakota and Montana most noticeable to a stranger is the soft, low tone in which conversation is carried on, together with the correct language and polite manners of the men. We were also quite surprised to find along our route a number of young Eastern society men, blossomed out as cowboys, who spend their summers on the ranches and their winters in New York, and combine the cowboy and dude in a most astonishing manner.

From St. Paul onward the climate changed decidedly. The air became purer and drier. The sun cast a sharp, black shadow like that of the electric light ; and however hot its rays might be, it was cool and comfortable in the shade, while the nights grew cooler and cooler.

No more comfortable trip can be imagined than that over the Northern Pacific. The road is comparatively new, and the cars are constructed with the modern improvements. A dining car is attached to each train on which meals can be eaten at leisure. The fruit was from California, so that both sections of the continent were represented at each meal. There is no dust, no alkali plains, and the cool nights insure a restful sleep.

The evening after we left St. Paul brought a marked change in temperature as we sped Northward. The air seemed clearer and more bracing. Morning showed a decided alteration in the scenery, which continued during the day. Trees gradually became scarcer and scarcer. Houses were more scattered, and the country began to flatten out into broad expanses of slightly rolling prairie land, extending on every side as far as the eye could reach.

Here the so-called " Bonanza Farms " were encountered, their vast wheat fields stretching on each side of the road for miles, and unbroken by a single fence ; an omission which gives a singular look to the landscape to Eastern eyes. Think of twenty-seven thousand acres in a single farm, and that equipped with quantities of the most improved machinery and managed as a general would handle a brigade! The head-quarters of these farms, with numerous large stables and other buildings, and the handsome house of the manager formed small villages. While these farms produce largely and pay well, (although as to the latter there is considerable dispute) the general opinion of the people appeared to be decidedly unfavorable to them, as detracting from the best interests of the State. For this reason, I was told that they sought to discriminate against them as much as possible in local taxation.

Every twenty or thirty miles we passed through a town. Some like Fargo are bustling, enterprising places, claiming a population of 10,000, with handsome buildings, telephones, electric lights and all the modern improvements. The great majority, however, consist of a line of one-story wooden buildings standing with their gable ends to the main street, which fronts on the railroad, the fronts being boarded across up to the ridge pole, so as to make them look flat-roofed. Intersperse among these a few one, or sometimes two-story brick stores, a hotel of such size as to induce the belief that all the population of the place must live there, and from twenty to fifty small houses scattered irregularly over the prairie behind the main street, and you have the typical Western town.

It must, however, have several saloons, a bank and one, and more often, two newspapers to be of any account. Trees, shrubbery and green vegetation of any kind are usually conspicuous by their absence.

The great event of the day in all these towns, particularly in the smaller ones, is the arrival of the two through trains (from the East and West). Everybody who can do so, comes down to the depot, and hangs around until the train leaves, to welcome new comers, take leave of those who are departing and to learn the news. In some of the places where the trains stop in the night-time, the effect is to turn day into night, as all hotels, saloons, etc., must be open at train time. The wheat country appeared to extend all through Minnesota, and through a large part of Dakota, and for all this distance and on each side of the track unfenced fields of grain extended for miles, the expanse rarely broken by the figure of a man or animal.

Just beyond Bismarck we crossed the Missouri, over a magnificent bridge, which cost $1,000,000, and in accordance with the rule of the road, all of the passengers went out on the platform to admire it.

This is more than we could do for the river, in fact it is a misnomer to call the Missouri a river at all. It is simply a stream of mud with just enough water to make it liquid. Its turbid, clay-colored flow, swirls and eddies with a swift current, between dreary flats of baked clay along the shore, and is broken by slimy bars projecting here and there in the channel. No sane person would dream of bathing in it, and to fall into it with one's clothes on is death. The banks are also constantly crumbling and falling, so that it is unsafe to build too near the edge, or to ford it.

We were now well into Dakota, and cattle began to take the place of wheat. The cattle, however were back on the ranges at this season. Occasionally, but not often, a "bunch" or two were to be seen. At last, however, we were rewarded with the sight of several "bunches" aggregating some thousand or more ; some of which were being "rounded up," by squads of four or five cowboys, in a most animated manner.

Subsequent experience led me to the belief that the passing train with its freight of ladies and "pilgrims," (*i. e.,* people from the East) had more to do with the

" round up " than any exigencies of the situation. But by whatever cause inspired, the cowboys galloped around the cattle like mad men, swinging their lariats over their heads, cutting out a steer here, and heading off another there, and riding as if they were superior to the influences of gravitation.

It is the rule for the men of the plains, and particularly for cowboys to speak most contemptuously of Eastern fashions and Eastern " dudes." But in fact, some of them are as much the slaves of fashion as any one. No man, who can by any possibility avoid it, engages in any part of the business of cattle raising, however subordinate, without first procuring a white felt hat with an immensely broad brim, and a band consisting either of a leather strap and buckle, or of a silk twist like a whip lash. These hats are expensive, like a fine Panama, frequently costing from fifteen to twenty-five dollars. A cowboy must also have a pair of fancy chapareros, or overalls, made out of calves skin, or stamped leather. Boots with high French heels are very popular. Our men all wore them, and when I compared them with my own shooting boots with broad soles and low flat heels, and I asked them why they wore such French affairs, I was told that there was no sale in Montana for boots with anything but French heels, and consequently few others were imported for cattlemen.

A red handkerchief doubled, the ends knotted around the throat and the rest streaming out over the shoulders, but adjusted a little to one side, is also *de rigeur* among the cattlemen. This is a good thing, as it keeps off the sun from the back of the neck and shoulders, while not excluding the air.

Many cowboys, particularly further south, spend a large part of their earnings in fancy ornaments for their pistols, such as carved ivory handles and gold mountings.

To the owner of a regulation hat, chapareros, boots, silk handkerchief and revolvers, the style and quality of the rest of his clothing is of little or no importance.

At Billings a thrill was experienced at the sight of several Indian tepees, the camp of Sitting Bull pitched by the river, with the genuine savages lounging in front of them. We also saw some emigrants slowly wending their way over the prairie with mule teams and huge canvass-covered wagons, the well-known " prairie schooner." Occasionally a settler's cabin would be seen. These were mostly "dug-outs" half cellar and half cave, banked up on the sides with logs and sods, the roof covered with earth, and overspread with a luxuriant growth of grass and flowers. Where the rafters of this style of edifice (which is usually known as a claim shack) are not strong, it is not uncommon for the occupants to be surprised by a grazing steer or horse " dropping in on them " through it.

These were scarcely passed when a prairie dog village was encountered. Its small occupants perched themselves upon the tops of their burrows as the train approached and uttered feeble barks of defiance, usually followed by a plunge into their holes. A passenger emptied his revolver at one of them from the train platform and returning, and complacently remarked to his bride, " I hit him," with the air of a conqueror. The pistol he used would not hit a flour barrel at the distance at which he fired, and the train was then going thirty miles an hour. Yet although a number of those who heard the remark were thoroughly familiar with shooting and the ways of prairie dogs, with the exception of a subdued smile and a wink, no one cast a doubt upon his assertion.

After passing Fryburgh the traveler finds himself amid that extraordinary country known as the " Bad Lands."

These seem to have been the scene of some vast convulsion of nature. Whether caused by the burning out

BAD LANDS.

of veins of coals, the washing out of a great lake, or some other geological occurrence is immaterial. The practical effect has been, that for some fifteen miles the surface of the country is broken into every conceivable shape. Now we would be passing through buttes fifty to one hundred and fifty feet high, with steep sides and rounded tops, the former marked by broad bands of color, some brilliant red, others black, or brown, alternated with stripes of all colors from gray to white. Next, we would pass a ravine full of petrified tree trunks, and then through a mass of towers and pinnacles of every conceivable shape and hue, some like mushrooms, others like pulpits. In the distance, and sometimes quite close to the track could be seen the smouldering fires of the burning veins of coal, sometimes breaking out into flames and making it unsafe to walk in their neighborhood.

Just beyond the Bad Lands we found ourselves in Montana, and had to put our watches back an hour from St. Paul time, as we now began to run on Mountain time. Here, for a long distance, the road followed the valley of the Yellowstone, along which we were to spend so many pleasant days.

It is a clear stream, swift as a mill-race and so full of eddies and whirlpools as to make it dangerous to navigate and still more dangerous to swim in. It is crossed by ferry-boats, which are attached to a rope geared to pulleys running on a wire rope stretched across the river. By adjusting those so as to bring the boat at an angle with the current it is carried over by its force, and without exertion from the ferryman.

The snowy crags of the Rocky Mountains, (the Snow Mountains and the Crazies) also begin to make their appearance, towering up like clouds against the sky, and from that time until our return we were scarcely ever out of sight of some of the snow-topped peaks of its various ranges.

Finally we reached Livingston from where the branch railroad extends to near the Park.

Most of our fellow-tourists left the cars here. These were few in number, as we were ahead of the season, and the hard times had lessened travel here as in the East.

CHAPTER III.

BOZEMAN.

We, however, continued to Bozeman, twenty-five miles further on where we quitted the cars, having made the journey of one thousand and fifty-seven miles from St. Paul in two days and nights with less fatigue than is usually experienced in going from New York to Chicago. We had decided to take our departure for the field from Bozeman, instead of from the Mammoth Springs, although it involved an extra ride of over two hundred miles, mainly because we hoped to induce some of the army officers from Fort Ellis to accompany us, and partly, because we desired the benefit of their advice and experience in laying our plans and choosing our outfit.

Bozeman is an older town than most of those that are met with on the line of the Northern Pacific, and is quite a pleasant place. As it is situated in a valley bordered by high mountains, and is reached by the railroad over what appears to the traveller to have been a level country, it is difficult to believe that it is four thousand feet above tide water, higher than the summit of most of the mountains in the East, and even than Vesuvius in Italy.

In fact, considering the altitudes of the Park and its neighborhood, it is well to bear in mind that Mount Marcy, the highest peak in the Adirondacks is but five thousand four hundred and two feet high, and Mount Washington six thousand four hundred and twenty-eight, while the Great Cañon is over eight thousand feet above the level of the sea.*

Although suffering a reaction from the boom which it experienced during the construction of the railroad, Bozeman seemed thriving. Many of the stores on its

---

* See table of elevation, on Page 245.

main street were of brick, and in fact, were larger and
better supplied than would be the case in an Eastern
place of its population.   The ladies bought some sun hel-
mets, mosquito netting and similar things, and found
them but very little dearer than in New York.   The
stores were full of fine fruit from Oregon and California,
particularly of plums.   The ladies bought a basket of the
latter, and were told that the price was two " bits."
They had not the slightest idea whether this was two
dimes or two dollars, and were too much ashamed of appearing ignorant to ask.   So they tendered a bill in payment, and were relieved to find by counting their change,
that " two bits " meant twenty-five cents.

There were quite a number of pleasant residences in
the borders of the town, and many trees and gardens,
kept green by irrigating ditches, which gave it to
Eastern eyes quite a homelike appearance.   The little
children seemed more fat and rosy than is usual in the
East, and were perpetually threatening to fall into
the irrigating ditches.   While there was a skating rink
with a brass band in full blast, the main amusement of
the young ladies of the town seemed to be riding on
horseback.   When the sun went down and the air began to
cool they swarmed out from every direction in couples or
parties, but usually without any masculine companion.

One fair equestrian in particular excited the admira-
tion and envy of the ladies in our party.   Young and
quite stout, she wore a riding habit of blue plush, and
rode a tall, bay mare, along side of which trotted a little
mule colt, wearing a broad yellow ribbon tied on its
shoulders in an enormous bow !   As the fair rider would
dash down the street in front of our hotel, with her blue
plush skirts streaming behind her, the little mule would
follow with his nose close up to them.   Every little while he
would stop, as little colts do, to investigate some strange
object along the side of the road, and then suddenly ob-

serving that his mother was leaving him, would burst
into a shrill whinny and an awkward gallop and tear
after her as fast as his long legs would carry him, his yellow ribbon flapping at every jump, making a most æsthetic spectacle.

The small boys of Bozeman appeared to spend their
spare time mostly on horseback. Their great delight was
to be able to dress in regular cowboy fashion, with
leather overalls and Mexican spurs. I noticed one, the
bridle and headstall of whose pony was composed of
twisted hair, red, white and blue, a cowboy luxury which
I was told, cost nearly a hundred dollars. The boys,
of course, rode at full gallop and through all the mud-
holes whenever there were any. How it was that they
never rode over any one in darting around the corners of
the streets as they did, I did not exactly understand, but
they did not seem to do it. One small youth, who be-
strode a restless little broncho, paid so little heed to the
laws of gravitation as to neglect to fasten his " chinch "
(i. e., saddle girth) the saddle being simply balanced on
the horse's back. When his attention was called to this
slight oversight, he merely remarked that he " knew it,"
and continued his wild career without attempting to
fasten it. I was told, however, that the influences of
towns like this on boys are not good, and that it was difficult for parents to properly control and bring them up.

We stopped at the Eastman House, which is very neatly
kept. It had no bar, and was therefore very quiet, more
like a boarding-house at a small watering place than a
hotel. It was papered in the latest æsthetic manner with
dados, friezes, etc. Here as in many other places in the
Far West, from the difficulty of getting proper lime for
white plaster, the ceilings and frequently the walls, even
of good houses are covered with unbleached cloth made
especially for the purpose. The wall paper s pasted directly upon this, so that it could not be told that it was

not plaster, except that it is a little startling at first to see the ceiling wave as if it was all coming down on the heads of those below. We realized, however, here that we were two thousand miles from New York, by finding that a modest "tip" to the girl that waited on us was met with the question, "What is that for?" and was then promptly declined.

In wandering around Bozeman we were startled to observe handbills posted all over, " *Vote for Miss Hamilton—The People's Choice.*"

It seems that in Montana not only does female suffrage exist in matters affecting the schools, but women are eligible for office. Miss Hamilton was a candidate for the position I believe of School Superintendent, and I was glad afterwards to learn was elected by a large majority. For this she seems to have been greatly indebted to her opponent. He had occupied the position for which she was candidate, for several years, and was enraged at the thought that a woman should have the audacity to oppose his re-election. In a speech made shortly before the election to a crowded meeting, composed largely of his own adherents, I was told, he forgot himself so much as to sneer at Miss Hamilton as "a school marm who had come into the territory a few years ago without a dollar in her pocket." He was continuing in this strain, when an Irishman in the audience started up and interrupted him by a stentorian shout—" Boys, let's give three cheers for Miss Hamilton;" whereupon every man in the audience stood up in his place, waved his hat and cheered for Miss Hamilton at the top of his lungs. What is more, on election day, they and most of the other men in the town voted for Miss Hamilton, thereby, as Sam, my informant told me, " showing what comes of abusing a woman in Montana."

CHAPTER IV.

FORT ELLIS.

In going through the streets of Bozeman blue uniforms were frequently met. These were worn by soldiers from Fort Ellis, an army post which is situated about three miles east of the town. Having letters to some of the officers, I drove there directly after our arrival at Bozeman, to learn what was the best course to adopt in securing an "outfit." Those unfamiliar with American army life, in reading a reference to "Fort Ellis" doubtless picture to their mind's eye some frowning fortification with high walls (or at the very least stockades) enclosing a fine grassy parade, on which long lines of brilliantly dressed troops are being constantly drilled, and around which are clustered elegant buildings, the residences of the officers and the barracks of the men.

The real Fort Ellis is a collection of rambling one-story log houses, so old and dilapidated that a prosperous farmer would think twice before using them for cow stables, (which were the barracks which this generous Government provides for its soldiers), a row of one-story, shabby little cottages (the quarters of the officers) and a few two-story administration buildings of comparatively respectable appearance. These were situated on a barren plateau scantily covered by a little coarse grass, but which to make up for it, was absolutely overrun with gophers, a dozen of which could be seen in a space fifty feet square. Neither trees, nor lawn, nothing in fact, was visible to break the monotony of the prairie, except the rugged peaks of Mount Bridger and the other mountains which hemmed in the valley, and which were really imposing in appearance. A few years since, the Indians were so daring that the Fort was palisaded, and it was dangerous to go two hundred yards from the gates. But there are no Indians now in this neighborhood, and the only fences now existing are a few to keep out the stray cattle of the garrison herd.

The ardor of the most enthusiastic would-be soldier would be dreadfully chilled by the mere appearance of the Fort, and would be destroyed by learning the life which those living there are forced to lead. On this arid spot, where for eight months in the year the snow lies upon the ground so that no out-door military instruction is practicable, and the thermometer falls to more than thirty degrees below zero, are stationed four companies of about thirty men each, and eight company officers. These officers and their families live together all their lives. While this unites them very closely it makes it difficult to find new topics of conversation, or to avoid stale stories. Moreover, while army ladies are very amiable and long suffering, they are still human, and disagreements occasionally occur between them, or between their children as between other neighbors, but with much more awkward results. This, however, is peculiar to all army life, and no one complains. But the great, disheartening factor is the absurdly small number both of officers and men. Out of the eight officers at a post like this, two are required for Adjutant, Quartermaster, etc., and with one on sick, or other leave, there remains but one officer to attend to all the affairs of each company, so that his entire time is taken up in the petty details of garrison life. It is even worse as far as the rank and file are concerned. The fatigue duties of the post require many details from each company for men to cut and draw wood, and do the other necessary work. Add to these those required for guards, the prisoners, etc., etc., and the single officer finds that he has not present for drill more than twelve men ! Of course, no military instruction worthy of the name is possible with a squad of this size ; neither is there any inducement for their commander to study the pro-

fession of arms, for proficiency will lead to no advance-
ment or reward, nor is there any opportunity for practis-
ing what is learned. In my judgment, it reflects the
greatest credit upon the officers of our army, who are
stationed on the frontier, that they do not become utterly
useless as soldiers, through the hopeless stagnation of
their life.

I have scarcely ever pitied a man more than I did one
who said to me with unconscious pathos : "I am fifty-
nine years of age, and have been in the army twenty-five
years, yet here I am, only a captain, with no chance of
promotion, and must turn out every day to drill a squad
of *twelve men.*"

In former times when Indian troubles were constant,
there was always a liability to be called into active service, and although Indian fighting is the hardest of hard
work, with little or no glory as a reward, yet the knowl-
ledge that it might come at any moment kept off the
monotony which now hangs like a pall over posts like
this. Then again, until recently, there was good hunting and fishing around the Fort, and field sports served
to alleviate garrison existence. Now, however, it is
necessary to go thirty to fifty miles for anything of the
kind. The Indians are distant and peaceable, and life at
the post is terribly dull. Rifle shooting is the one thing
in which all are interested. This brings the officers and
men into competition with each other, and with the different organizations of the army, and they consequently
give to it an amount of thought and time which would
astonish the National Guardsman of the East, over
whom, however, they have the great advantage of leisure
and unlimited ammunition. By four o'clock in the
morning the men at Fort Ellis were at the butts and the
practice was continued all day long. No lady was ever
keener to know the last fashions than the officers there
were to get new ideas as to how to improve the shooting

of themselves and their men. In consequence, the officers and men of the army are becoming really wonderful marksmen, not only at fixed targets, but as skirmishers.

CHAPTER V.

OUR OUTFIT AND DEPARTURE.

In true western style, a Bozeman gentleman who had learned on the cars our proposed trip, although a stranger, laid aside his business to aid us. Soon, under his inspiration, quite a considerable portion of the population of Bozeman were engaged in canvassing as to what men were suitable for our purposes, and where they were to be found. On the suggestion that Jack Somebody and his partner had come in town, and were just the men we wanted, we started to hunt them up. We soon found them, peacefully camped in the eastern end of the town, on the side of a street. Here they had pitched a dingy little A tent, around which their horses were picketed, and were cooking their dinner as comfortably as if on the prairie. Unfortunately, they had arranged to start on a prospecting tour and could not go with us, but they thought "Jim Fisher" would, and if he would he was just the man we wanted.

After a few inquiries we found Fisher, tending bar in a lager beer saloon. It was not exactly the place from which to select a guide, but I liked his looks. He was willing to accompany us, and produced such high recommendations from previous employers, that I engaged him on the spot. It was a fortunate selection. We found him to be what he was represented, a thoroughly honest and reliable man, without a lazy hair in his head, familiar with the Park and the surrounding country, a good hunter and mountaineer, and what was still more important, as there were ladies in the party, a man who was quiet and gentlemanly in his manners. He was one of the few guides I have had who did not want to do all the shooting himself, but always gave his employer all the chances. For sixteen dollars a day, he gave his own services and provided his own saddle and horse and one for me, a four-horse wagon driven by "Sam" C. King, his partner, who also acted as cook, and an assistant, Horace Cleveland. This included forage for the work horses, the saddle ponies grazing. All the men were the best type of Western frontiersmen—quiet, self-respecting, obliging and always respectful. They knew their work thoroughly and did it well, and while they expected to be treated as equals and were so treated, there was no attempt at undue familiarity. Throughout all the trip not a vulgar word or coarse expression was uttered by either of them in our hearing. They had each spent the best part of their lives on the plains, and although not given to boasting were full of curious and interesting reminiscences. Sam in particular was full of dry wit and quaint sayings which made him very good company.

Besides the outfit provided by Fisher I hired two saddle horses for the ladies from a Bozeman ranchman, for a dollar a day each, making the cost of the outfit eighteen dollars a day, which was not dear for such a large party.

Both the work and saddle horses were "Cayuses," i. e., a cross between the Mustang and American horse. It is the habit in the West to speak disrespectfully of the "Cayuse;" and considering how cruelly they are apt to be treated, it is not surprising that they are sometimes vicious. Acting on the principle that they are irredeemably bad, the most severe measures are resorted to upon the least sign of opposition or disobedience, thus, (in my humble opinion), frightening the animals and making them "cantankerous."

For my own part, I have nothing but good to say of those we had to deal with. My own horse got to be quite a pet. He would eat out of my hand, stand, when I dismounted to shoot, and walk over the steepest and most broken paths, without a thought of stumbling, where an ordinary horse would either never have ventured or would have broken his own or his rider's neck if he had, and would gallop over a prairie full of gopher and badger holes without dreaming of stepping into one. Our other horses were almost as reliable. In fact, my wife, whose nerves had been so much shaken by the up-setting of a carriage some years since as to cause her to be timid in all matters connected with horses, soon got so that she would ride her pony without a tremor over a trail like a sheep path, winding down the precipitous side of a deep cañon. Her horse was a one-eyed white animal with a very gentle gait, and was known as "Old Riley." He had no vices or tricks, except that he must have been brought up in a country abounding in rattlesnakes, which had led him to form the habit of half squatting and then making a little rush whenever a grasshopper would set up a sharp buz-z-z close to his heels. As grasshoppers were numerous, this habit was a source of numerous surprises to his rider. Whether from his limited vision or not, he was always having some accident or other happening to him, carrying out the fatality which our men insisted always attached to white horses. My daughter's cayuse rejoiced in the name of "Daisy." Her owner told us it was given her by a lady in appreciation of her merits ; while her gaits were easy she varied them constantly, and our men after riding her, declared that her name had been bestowed in some sarcastic moment by a disgusted rider. All the other horses used to try to ingratiate themselves into her good graces, but she was a complete coquette. She had a happy knack of going ahead on three legs and kicking a too attentive companion with the fourth, and it made no difference to her in doing this at what pace she was going, or whether it suited the feelings of her rider. She was always gentle to the latter, to whom she afforded more than enough amusement to compensate for her tricks, although Fisher, who saddled her, was probably of a different opinion.

Fisher made up a list of the supplies required, which I checked off from a list I had myself prepared, and it was quite curious how closely they corresponded. We bought all our supplies at Bozeman, and were surprised at the reasonable prices and good quality of the articles we obtained. For instance, we paid for canned corned beef thirty-five cents; the same price for California peaches (better than those obtained in the East), flour two dollars and sixty-five cents for a hundred pounds, cartridges one dollar and fifteen cents a box, and other things in the same proportion. In the shooting line the sportsman can obtain almost anything he wants as well at Bozeman as at home, as it possesses one of the best gun stores in the West.

Our friends among the army officers at Fort Ellis vied with each other in helping us to secure our outfit. Everything that they had, buffalo robes, blankets, camp stoves, overcoats, etc., etc., were pressed upon us with that generosity which is so characteristic of army officers, until we were fairly obliged to decline further loans for want of transportation.

One of the officers had obtained leave of absence to accompany us when, with the pleasing uncertainty so characteristic of army life, orders came to hold the cavalry companies in readiness to march instantly; the Cheyenne difficulty having assumed serious proportions. We waited several days in the hope that these orders would be countermanded, and we could have the pleasure of being accompanied by some of our friends from the Fort, but in vain, and so on July 13, we left Bozeman and started alone on our journey. Our supplies consisting of bacon, canned corned beef, tongue, and peaches, sardines, lager beer, etc., were contained in the wagon. This was a heavy "dead ex" freight wagon drawn by four horses, driven by Sam, while Horace handled the brakes. It was a mistake to have taken such a heavy vehicle, as a far lighter one would have been more useful. I would advise those contemplating a similar trip to take two light covered wagons, each drawn by two horses, one to carry the tents and provisions, the other, some of the personal effects, but having room for some of the party to ride in, in case they should become fatigued. This would require no more men or horses, and involve no more expense, and would add much to the comfort of the party. We saw two parties from Bozeman in the Park, each of which was as large as ours, and yet each had but one wagon, an ordinary covered grocer's cart, and they seemed to get on quite comfortably.

I carried my canvas shooting jacket and overalls tied in a roll at the back of the saddle, and all of us had a waterproof tied either to the pommel or cantle. Those of our personal effects which we were likely to need every night were kept in three valises in the back of the wagon, and the ladies' toilet articles in two little satchels under the driver's seat. The rest of our clothing was in a single trunk. My ammunition was in a small canvas bag under the driver's seat. The provisions were packed in wooden boxes and the beer in the regular cases. All these were stowed firmly together in the wagon bottom, the rolls of bedding and blankets put over them, then the tent, and finally, the canvas wagon cover was drawn together and tied. We never lost a thing out of the wagon, except upon one occasion shortly after our departure.

This was the valise that contained all the fishing tackle, a loss which spread silent horror among the party, until Horace rode back and found it lying in the trail over which we had come. We had two tents—a wall tent for our own party, and a small A tent belonging to the men.

Our train presented an odd appearance, that would have attracted a large audience on Broadway. Usually I rode in advance, partly because my pony was the fastest at the "lope" and the slowest at a walk, and next to look out for game, accompanied by my daughter. Then came my wife and Fisher, and then our four-horse wagon, with cover once white but now gray, and a driver and brakeman of heterogeneous apparel, whose cries of encouragement or reproach to their horses at each heavy grade were shrill and continuous. The ladies wore short travelling dresses with pantaloons under them, and heavy high shoes. One had a white cork helmet with a vail twisted around it, the other a broad felt hat with a similar vail, the former being by far the best for the purpose. My own equipment, although not picturesque, was so comfortable that I doubt if I could improve upon it. A Chinese pith helmet, varnished with shellac to keep out the rain, a Norfolk jacket (a kind of loose plaited sack with plenty of pockets), heavy gray pantaloons, canvas leggings, broad soled shoes and a cartridge belt of webbing. The latter will be found a great comfort where day after day is to be spent in the saddle by those who are unaccustomed to it, as it supports the abdomen and prevents fatigue. My rifle I carried in hunter fashion —*i. e.*, hung horizontally along the left side of the horse, the barrel passing under the saddle flap and left knee, the muzzle through a socket in the rear of the saddle flap, and the stock embraced in the loop of a strap that went over the pommel. This is by far the most convenient way of carrying a gun when mounted. It never catches in brush or rocks, does not disturb one's horse, and can be got at quickly when wanted.

To intending travelers, however, I may say, that if they only propose to go through the Park, no fire-arms are needed. In the first place, it is strictly against the law to shoot anything ; and in the second, there is nothing to shoot, as the travel on the main road, as a rule, keeps all game at a distance. Twice in the Park we saw fresh antelope tracks in the road, but one solitary coyote and a jackass rabbit were the only wild creatures we actually met. Others, however, were more fortunate.

Outside the Park both a rifle and shotgun are needed.

I carried a 45-75 Winchester repeating rifle, and I wish for no better weapon.* It has, of course, the disadvantage of having higher trajectory than an Express rifle, or those using a heavier charge of powder and a lighter bullet ; but this can be largely controlled by the proper use of the front sight, and is compensated for by a longer range. Still there is but little game killed at over 200 yards distance.

I used the Freund sights, which I consider the best for sporting. In these, the front sight consists of a rib of tempered steel, something like the crescent sight upon an old-fashioned Kentucky rifle, but higher, and beveled at the sides so as to give the effect of a pin-head when seen from the rear. It looks slight, but will stand rough usage. It may bend, but it will not stay bent or break. It has a white centre and dark shoulders, so that it can be seen clearly in taking aim under all circumstances. This is effected by inlaying a strip of white metal in the lower end of the front sight, the top of which is cut at such an angle as to reflect the light, making it, when seen from the rear, present the appearance shown in the cuts on page 40, which are numbered 1, 2 and 3. These represent the different styles of beads which are used,

* See remarks on hunting rifles, page 229.

No. 1, a white pin with a black centre, being intended for
fine target work ; No. 2 for target or field work, and
No. 3 (having the largest bead), specially for hunting.
These are made, if desired, so as to fit into the same
block without moving the latter. The rear sight re-
sembles somewhat the well-known "buck horn," but has
a pear-shaped opening in its base. The aim, however, is
not taken through this aperture, but through the notch
above it, as shown in the lower right-hand cut.

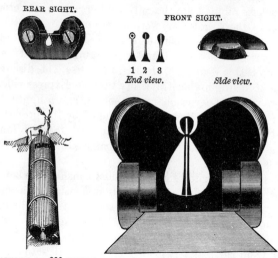

REAR SIGHT.

FRONT SIGHT.

1   2   3
End view.

Side view.

AIMING AT 600 YARDS.

AIMING AT 100 YARDS.

These sights show bright on a dark background, and
dark on a light one. They are almost the only sights I know
of which can be accurately drawn in aiming so as to give
the desired elevation. On my rifle drawing the pin-head
as fine as possible gave me "point blank" for fifty feet,
a most important distance, by-the-by, for if a sportsman
ever has to shoot at that distance he will need to hit inside of the size of a dollar, and most rifles are sighted so
as to carry several inches over it at it. Taking in the whole

of the pin-head gave the elevation for 100 yards ; dividing the sight equally that for 200 and taking in the whole sight down to the barrel 300 yards. These divisions are difficult to make upon an ordinary sight but are easily made upon this, as you can see the portion of the front sight which is below as well as that which is above the line of the rear sight, and so calculate with exactness. The opening in the rear also cuts off all blur and gives great distinctness to the view of the front sight. I have had small silver bars inlaid across the barrel of my rifle, and raised just enough above its surface to make a line which is visible from the rear. These are respectively at about $8\frac{1}{4}$, $11\frac{1}{4}$, $13\frac{1}{4}$, and $15\frac{1}{4}$ inches from the front sight, and represent the elevations for 400, 500, 600 and 700 yards, respectively. In using them, *the butt of the rifle is lowered* until the top of the rear sight is on a level with the bar desired (which gives the muzzle the same elevation as if the rear sight had been elevated and the front sight raised to a level with it). Then, keeping that elevation, the point of the front sight is put on the mark and the trigger pulled. In firing at a long distance, the first shot should always be fired a little under the estimated distance. If the rifle is reloaded rapidly, the second shot can be taken almost the instant the first is seen to strike, and if the latter falls short or over, the necessary alteration can be made with accuracy by this method of aiming without altering the sights. The advantage is that a shot may be fired instantly at any distance from fifty feet to 700 yards without touching the rear sight. For large game I used the " Keene " bullet, sold by the Winchester Arms Company. It is a bullet having two saw cuts at right angles and which extend from its point to nearly where it enters the shell. These are then swedged up so as to be imperceptible. The impact of the ball when fired against anything solid bends these points backward, forming a four pointed star, giving a crushing blow and the whirl of the bullet makes them cut like an auger, tearing a fearful hole. An elk struck by one falls as if hit by a sledge hammer. Nothing that 1 hit with one ever went twenty feet afterwards.

The sportsman who goes to the Great West needs the most powerful rifle he can get, as the game is large and hard to kill. If he is going for bear he must be sure of himself as well as his rifle ; and above all be certain how the latter carries at close quarters. Few appreciate how much the ordinary rifle overshoots at short distances, and how apt one is, for that reason, to miss. Some people talk about walking up to a grizzly and putting a bullet between his eyes at ten paces. If you have the nerve and skill to do it, it is all right, but failure is death. I knew of one man, who was armed with a rifle like mine (but using the ordinary bullet), who fired at a grizzly when 100 yards off. The bear rushed for him and he fired seven shots, while bruin was covering the distance, but although every one hit in a vital place, the bear was not stopped until the very last, a fortunate shot in the head dropped him when not ten feet from the hunter. Only the latter's wonderful nerve saved his life. Another bear, with two Express bullets through his heart, made a rush up a hill at his assailant, and the sportsman's life was only preserved by a lucky shot which broke the animal's foreshoulder and swerved him from his path ; he lived for some moments afterwards, time enough to have torn the hunter to pieces. Some of the coolest and best riflemen I know have refused to fire at a grizzly when alone, and in such close proximity that they had a chance for but a single shot. For my own part, although very anxious to kill a bear, and having a reasonable degree of confidence in my own nerves and skill, as well as in the power of my rifle, I was not at all desirous of having a single combat with one under the circumstances in which Mr. Roosevelt kills his bears. As an army friend of mine said, " I value a grizzly's hide, but not enough to bet my life against it." With fifty or sixty yards clear space so as to be able to get in several shots, it would, however, be another thing. But even then, no one should try it unless he knows he can shoot fast and straight, when under the excitement incident to a grizzly's coming for him like a tornado.

In the wagon I carried a twelve-bore shot-gun. This had an auxiliary rifle barrel, carrying a Winchester 44-50 cartridge. This is a short rifle barrel made to fit one of the shot barrels, and which slips into the latter like a cartridge and has an extractor which is actuated by the extractor of the gun itself. A little practice is required to learn how to shoot with it. If used in the right barrel, the aim should be from the right edge of the rib to the fore sight. If in the left, the aim must be over the left edge of the rib, as the shot barrels incline inward ; when the proper method to use it was learned, we could break a bottle with it at sixty yards every time. I carried shells for my twelve-bore loaded with No. 6, 4 and 2 shot and a few with buckshot. Besides the rifle and twelve-bore, Fisher took along a little .22 calibre rifle for the ladies to shoot with, which we frequently found quite handy in shooting birds and small game.

The Eastern rider who starts out for a long ride upon a Mexican saddle, will find it much more comfortable to make a change in his manner of riding. I am not positive whether or not the stirrups upon this kind of saddle are actually set further back than upon an English saddle, but they seem to be so. At all events, for comfort in a long trip, they should be worn so long that when the foot is resting in them the toe is slightly lower than the heel. The body ought to be relaxed, so as to sway with each movement of the horse, and the riding be by balance more than by the grip of the thighs, all of which tends to avoid fatigue. Care must be taken not to allow the knees to become stiff, for this does not seem to wear off, if once established, as is the case with fatigue of other muscles. It is therefore wise, particularly upon first starting out, to dismount after riding a few hours and walk for five minutes until any stiffness in the knees is gone. It is well to remember that, if your horse does not lead well, you should not try to pull him forward by the reins, as he has the advantage of you if you attempt it. You should stand at his shoulder, grasp the reins close to his mouth and push him forward, and if he hangs back, switch his hind legs with your whip. The riding is all done with a powerful curb, no snaffle being used. The single rein is held loosely, usually suspended by the finger passed through a loop in it, and the horse is guided by pressure on the neck. The cowboys cross their reins under the horse's jaw, so that pressing the right rein on the neck pulls the horse's head to the left. Spurs are a nuisance, as they are in the way when dismounting. A whip is far preferable. The suggestion as to lengthening the stirrups and dismounting is as applicable to ladies as to gentlemen. Side saddles are very hard on horses in a country like this, and care should be taken to see that those used fit the horse that is to carry them. They should have two girths and be examined before starting out, so it can be known that they are strong and in good order. No horse should be taken for ladie's use, or in fact at all, whose back shows old saddle sores.

Leaving Fort Ellis, our route ran through Rocky Cañon, the pass through which the Northern Pacific reaches the Gallatin valley. Narrow, and overhung with beetling crags of soft terra cotta, grays and browns, which towered far upward, each turn opened a new scene before us. The narrow road, cut in the side of the mountains, constantly turned and twisted, at one moment running along the railroad track, then climbing upward, passed over a bluff, or crept around the edge of the cañon in a way calculated to disturb the nerves of a "pilgrim." Over this path our saddle ponies passed with a sure-footedness that soon inspired the ladies with confidence, and enabled them to face with equanimity the more serious precipices we subsequently encountered. As we rode across a little brook we were quite surprised to encounter a gentleman and his wife who had been staying at the hotel, who had ridden out to fish, and the adieus they waved were the last we saw of our Bozeman friends for many a day. I was a good deal troubled in passing through this cañon. The railroad track was always in sight, and at times quite close to our road. The afternoon train was due. The pole horses on the wagon were colts, only two months from the prairie; the saddle-horses were new to their riders, and I felt considerable anxiety as to how they might act if a train was to go by while we were in some dangerous portion of the road. It was therefore a great relief when after a few miles travel we left the cañon and turned south through a narrow but picturesque gap between the mountains. Here Daisy gave us the first example of her feminine caprices, by stopping when fording a stream until she was surrounded by the other horses, and then pawing the water until she had given them and her rider a good splashing. But this, however, soon dried. After riding through this cañon until about four o'clock, we went into camp at Hodson's Creek, having ridden thirteen miles, which was as much as we deemed it wise to travel on the first day of our trip.

CHAPTER VI.

CAMP LIFE.

The routine of camping was always the same, and with experience soon became rapid. During the day we would decide where we would camp for the night, the selection depending first upon getting good water, and next, upon finding suitable grazing for the stock. As we approached the place selected, Fisher would gallop on and reconnoiter, while we followed more slowly. We would find him waiting for us on what he considered the best spot.

"Well, what do you think of this?" he would ask, as we rode up. "This is all right," I would answer. "Pitch our tent *there*, fronting the east ; halt the wagon *there*, and place the table *there*." Those brief directions given, we would dismount, throwing the reins over our ponies' heads. This is almost equivalent to tying them, as they step on the reins and hurt their mouths with the curb if they attempt to walk.

The ladies would seek the nearest shade and lay themselves flat on their backs, the true way to rest (an idea which they had extracted from Mrs. Custer's "Boots and Saddles"), without much regard to the character of the ground, which however was always dry and warm, while Fisher and I would unsaddle the ponies, piling the saddles in a heap, and throwing the saddle-blankets over them to air and dry.

The wagon by this time would be up and would swing into the designated position and unharness. Fisher and Horace would lead the horses to the best grass. Those most inclined to stray would be picketed, the others hobbled. In picketing, a horse is fastened to each end of a rope sixty feet long, by a bowline knot around the throat. To the middle of this another rope is fastened, and at-

CAMPING IN THE YELLOWSTONE.

tached to a stout stake, tree or rock. This is decidedly preferable to picketing each animal separately. The horses are more quiet in each other's company, and if they do break away from the picket pin and stray off, are apt to bring up by the cross rope catching in a tree or rock. Besides the rope makes a trail which is easily followed. In hobbling, a leather strap about eighteen inches long is fastened to each foreleg. I prefer picketing to hobbling, as the latter affects a horse's gait.

While the horses were being put out, Sam would start his fire and put his Dutch oven into it to heat. This was a cast-iron kettle, with a cover of similar material turned up at the edges so as to hold embers, and proved to be a most indispensable article. While it was heating, he would wash his hands with great ostentation, (for the benefit of the ladies) retire into the wagon and mix his biscuit. By the time this was done, Horace would be back from the horses. He would put on more wood, fish out and grease the oven. The dough would then be put into the former, the cover put on and the whole affair placed in a bed of hot embers, which were also heaped over it. A large gridiron two feet square would then be set over the fire on which the other kettles and pans would soon be simmering; Sam flying around from one side of the fire to another, with an intense air of preoccupation, and occasionally uttering a droll remark regarding his experiences in cooking under the various circumstances of his checquered life. As soon as the bread was on the fire our tent would be put up. We always pitched this to face the East, so as to secure the warm rays of the morning sun when dressing, as this would warm the tent even though it might still be cold outside. The tent was put up by Fisher and Horace, with more or less help from me. We first pegged the corners and put up the pins for the corner guy ropes. Then we spread the tent, one of the men crawling into it and adjusting the poles, (presenting a most ludicrous appearance as he did so), raised it, tightened the corner guys and drove the other pins, and put a few stones on the flaps if the weather was cold, so as to keep the wind from blowing under it. The bedding was then unrolled, a large waterproof spread upon the ground, with two buffalo robes and then our three mattresses placed over them. The blankets were next spread, one over each mattress and four (?) for a cover. If the mosquitoes threatened to be troublesome, some sticks were put at the head of the beds and our mosquito nets tied to them ; but this precaution was but seldom necessary. The handbags were now carried into the tent and the camp was completed, the whole operation not occupying fifteen minutes. The men had an A tent which they only pitched when it was cold or threatened to rain. Usually they slept on the saddle blankets and used the tent as an extra covering.

Sam would have his bread baked in twenty minutes. He would then take it out, clean his Dutch oven, put in whatever he had to roast and put it back into the fire.

By the time the tent was up, the ladies had become sufficiently rested, and would begin to either sketch or read until the melodious banging of a tin pail and Sam's eloquent cry of "*Din-nur-r*" would rouse all to their feet. No one was ever late to dinner on that trip.

Our appetites were always enormous and not fastidious ; but as Sam was as neat as wax and a good cook, we fared well. The meals consisted of bread, game or fish when we had it, (and we generally had one or the other) bacon, canned corned beef, or tongue, baked beans, with sardines, pickles and potatoes ; and for dessert canned peaches or stewed apples and prunes. We always had delicious coffee free from all grounds, which we made by grinding the berry very fine, putting it into an unbleached muslin bag and pouring boiling water through it.

After dinner, the ladies would usually rest in a hammock, which was put up on the arrival of the wagon, (if there were any trees to tie it to) or sit around chatting, sometimes mending the clothes torn during the day and reading, while I would go fishing, if fishing was to be had. Although it was light enough to read up to half past nine o'clock, we usually went to bed at that hour, as it was important to make an early start to get over as much ground as possible before the heat of the day.

As the sun went down, the air rapidly grew chilly. I never wore an overcoat, but we dressed ourselves for the night as if in the Arctic regions ; of course, needing the most clothes in the highest altitudes, as near the Great Cañon. The ladies put on a pair of woolen stockings in place of those worn during the day, a suit of winter flannels over their others, a flannel skirt with a silk-lined flannel shoulder-cape forming a dress waist, an ulster, and a "Red Ridinghood" which reached to their waists. I changed my woolen stockings, substituted a heavy pair of drawers for my pantaloons, and a knit cardigan jacket for vest and coat, and with the aid of these few coverings and four blankets we managed to keep comfortable until morning. If it was unusually cold we spread our water-proofs on top of our blankets.

The men spread the saddle blankets a short distance from our tent and lay on them, covering themselves with their own blankets and usually with their tent, having a heavy revolver handy. They slept very lightly, and at short intervals one or the other would sit up and peer around to see if the horses were all right. The least sign of uneasiness on the part of any of the latter, a snort or stamp would bring all of the men to their feet like lightning. In a trip like this, the horses are the point on which everything turns, and they were seldom out of the mind of the men, particularly in the night-time. In fact, our first thought at all times was, "where are the horses?" All of our men had spent years watching horses on the prairie, and he would have been a skillful horse thief who could have got away with any of our stock.

The men rose at five o'clock; if the weather was cold, Horace made a brush fire in front of the tent and opened its flaps for a few minutes so as to warm the interior, while the other men would look up the horses. This was a very uncertain operation. Sometimes they would be found without trouble and act like lambs. Oftentimes some of them would be missing and have to be followed. Occasionally they objected somewhat to being bridled, but when this was once accomplished, they usually gave no farther trouble. I then struggled into my clothes and left the ladies to go through the double and complicated process of undressing and dressing for the day. Breakfast was ready about half past six; when it was ended, Sam would set a batch of biscuit to cook for lunch and begin to clean up.

While this was going on we packed our bags, put away our fishing tackle and folded the blankets. Horace and I then rolled the mattresses in the water-proof sheet, and the blankets in a buffalo robe and strapped both. The tent was then struck and after a careful scrutiny of the ground to see that nothing had been overlooked, the ladies, Fisher and myself rode off, leaving Sam and Horace to pack their wagon and follow when ready.

CHAPTER VII.

THE RIDE TO THE PARK.

Our first night's experiences of camp were novel in many respects, although none of us were strangers to camp life. We slept a dreamless but restful sleep and set off in the morning before nine o'clock. All felt inspirited by the pure air and beautiful scenery. Even the horses seemed to feel stimulated and stepped off briskly. The road was excellent. It followed up the cañon, and wound along its side a short distance above the brook which ran through its centre. The cañon itself was not as grand as Rocky Cañon through which we had passed the previous evening, but was more beautiful. Each open space we met was covered with vast quantities of tall, wild flowers thickly scattered along the high grass, and of such vivid hues as to cause constant exclamations of delight from the ladies who kept their belts full of fresh bouquets, which from time to time they plucked from their saddles as they rode along. Frequently these banks of flowers would extend from the ravine below us far up on the hills on either side. Whole fields of larkspur shoulder high, and great clusters of wild rose bushes were often met, while acres of other unknown but bright colored flowers rapidly succeeded each other. These flower-clad hills and slopes contrasting with the dark purple of the mountains formed a picture which never will be forgotten.

Being anxious not to tire the ladies before they became accustomed to the saddle, as well as desirous of enjoying this unusual sight, we rode most of the time at a walk so as just to keep ahead of the wagon, occasionally letting our horses "lope" for a mile or so. After some two

hours ride we emerged from the cañon and found ourselves in a desolate looking country. On either hand
high mountains lent an air of grandeur to the scene,
but the ground between them was a barren waste of
bare hills, bordering a rolling prairie sparsely covered
with scattered patches of bunch grass, a prospect which
seemed the more dreary after the banks of beautiful
flowers through which we had been riding. The season was now at hand when the prairie grass begins to
cure and turn yellow, and we could now see it change
day by day, keeping green the longest where there was
shade and moisture. Here we encountered alkali dust
for the first time. It was not as bad as it is found in
many places in the West, but nevertheless it was far from
agreeable. By noon we had made eleven miles and rested
at a brook. The ground was bare and baked as hard as
a brick and the sun was blazing hot. So long as we were
in motion we did not mind it, but when we halted, we
found it almost insupportable. We tried to get in the
shade of the wagon, but the sun was so vertical that
there was not enough shade to cover us, so we were compelled to improvise a shelter by a blanket thrown over
two poles. As soon as we could get out of the direct
rays of the sun we found the air as usual, quite cool and
comfortable.

On starting, after an hour's rest, those on saddle horses
left the hot and dusty road which followed the arid valley, and took a "short cut" of several miles over the
hills. This was one of the pleasures of travelling on
horseback. The scenery became beautiful as soon as we
got away from the road. Now we passed over a rolling
prairie, variegated with frequent buffalo skeletons and
occasional Indian graves (our route having been the scene
of the battle of Trail Creek, a fierce conflict between two
tribes), or skirted the craters of extinct volcanoes, some
bare and empty, and others converted into little ponds;

and now winding along an old buffalo trail, down the face of a steep bluff, with scarcely room for a horse to place his feet, and where our ponies had to clamber like goats over places were the path had been carried away. This whole country had been once so traveled by buffalo that the side hills were all cut up with their trails. Quite an industry has been carried on in collecting their bones, great piles of which could be seen piled up at the stations along the railroad which we passed during our journey from St. Paul. This, of course, makes them less frequent on the prairie than was formerly the case. In many places on the prairie and side hills large cactus were growing of vivid and varied color, yellow, orange and pink, which gave an almost theatrical effect to eyes as unused to them as ours. Presently we reached a prairie dog town ; a barren waste, with little mounds every twenty feet, the space around each being worn bare. On each of these sat a prairie dog, the image of self-complacency, barking his little squeaky bark until we got too near, when whiff! he disappeared head first into his domicile. I tried to shoot one, partly to see what he was like, but more to learn how much the wonderfully pure air would affect my estimate of distance. I found that one at first underestimates the distance by a third, and then is apt to go to the opposite extreme. It is no easy matter to hit a prairie dog, or at least to get him ; they are small ; you have to shoot from a distance, and they are apt to fall into their holes if hit. It was not until the fourth shot that I succeeded, although several times I felt certain that my shots had taken effect. This time I used a " Keene " bullet, which knocked the little fellow two feet in the air and away from his hole, and left little of him but his back and legs. They are curious creatures, a compromise between a gopher and a rabbit.

In this valley we met our first band of cattle, scattered over the prairie in little clumps. The cabin of the ranch seemed but a short distance off when we descended into the valley, but we rode an hour and a half before we reached it. After passing this ranch, we pushed on so as to reach Eight Mile Creek at its junction with the Yellowstone, where we arrived at five o'clock, making twenty-three miles in all, no small ride for a second day.

This creek was a beautiful little stream, running through a belt of cotton-wood, and was deliciously cool. It was a very desirable camping ground, and we had traveled farther to reach it than was quite wise, as the ladies had felt the heat considerably towards the close of the day. While putting out the horses, Fisher came upon a flock of willow grouse. I went over to where he was, but for want of a dog could find but two ; one of which I brought down with my shot-gun, the other flying behind Fisher's head, so that I dared not shoot. The others skulked in the grass and would not rise After supper I went down to the Yellowstone and tried my flies upon the trout. To my great surprise, I found that twilight continues so long in these high altitudes that I was able to fish until a quarter past nine, and then had light enough to return by. I made a good catch, the trout running from half a pound to a pound and a half, and rising freely to a " yellow coachman " and " red ibis."

During our stay at this camp, the ladies committed an indiscretion from which they suffered for several days. From the heat of the last hours of the march, their faces had become sunburned, which was quite unusual with them, they being brunettes. The shade and coolness of the creek were so delightful that they not only washed the dust off their faces with soap, but sat under the trees and bathed their faces for a long time during the evening. Now water, and above all, soap, should not be used upon a sunburned face, particularly in an alkali country, and the result was that their skins were greatly irritated for several days. Cuticura and Extract of Witch-hazel did little towards relieving them.   But when we were subsequently joined by Dr. L——, an application of oxide of zinc speedily removed all further annoyance.   All tourists should remember that until the face becomes toughened, a little washing goes a great way, and the less soap used upon it the better.   Although usually burning brick color with an exposure by which the ladies would not be affected, I was not annoyed as they were, which I ascribed to having bathed my face less than they did.   Neither Indians nor army officers during a campaign wash their faces at all, if it is either very hot or very cold.

The next day's ride of twenty-three miles took us through "Paradise Valley," a long, narrow valley, occupied by ranches and skirted by lofty mountains, their tops streaked with patches of snow, although the sun shone so hotly that it seemed impossible that it could remain.   Their faces clearly showed the grinding marks of glaciers, which had scooped out the rock like great planes, for miles at a time.   About noon we experienced our first and only rain-storm.   Heavy clouds gathered over the mountains, but only to pass off on either side. We could see the showers falling on the peaks and mountain sides all around, yet fancied we were to escape.   But a dark cloud swept up a cañon on the right, accompanied by a cold wind that instantly lowered the temperature twenty degrees, and then the storm struck us.   The behavior of our saddle horses was very amusing, and showed their prairie life plainly.   The moment they felt the cold storm they turned their backs around towards it and dropped their heads, and it took no little urging to induce them to proceed, as at each gust they would whirl their tails toward it as if turned by a crank.   Fortunately we were close to the log house of an original settler, who, having become rich, was building himself a palatial barn and frame house, and who treated us with the hospitality one always receives in the Far West.   His log cabin was flat roofed and not more than seven feet high. It was sparsely furnished, but its windows were filled with beautiful house plants. As the cabin was crowded, we took possession of the new barn, which had stalls for ten horses and room for three or four wagons, and there ate our lunch. By the time we had finished, the weather had cleared up. The fall in the temperature was remarkable. It was explained, however, by looking at the mountains around us, the peaks of which had perceptibly whitened, showing that what with us had been rain was snow above.

As we approached the end of this valley, it became more and more sterile. The ground was baked and the grass scant and coarse. Here and there were little marshes, each surrounding a pool, the white incrustations around which, as if lime had been strewed there, showed the presence of alkali in the water. A number of cattle were feeding close to these pools, as if they rather liked the flavor.

A stream sweeps across the valley near its end, which we forded. The water was up to our horses bellies, and was so swift that they had hard work to stem it and to keep their footing. The water was cold and looked pure, but although our horses were tired, they would not more than taste it, and we were content to trust to their instinct and imitate their example.

There was quite a comfortable ranch near this stream, which showed the steps of the settler's prosperity. First came the original little "claim shack," built of sods, now used as a store-house, then a small, one-room log-cabin with flat roof, now used as a stable, and then came a pretentious log-house with a peaked roof, and with as many as three rooms, (each one of which was larger than the old cabin,) in which the now affluent ranchman resided. There was also a garden with considerable shrubbery, and a little child was playing on the porch of the house.

A short ride further brought us to the entrance into Lower Cañon of the Yellowstone, where we had expected to camp, but found trouble in finding a suitable spot. The cañon was so deep that we could not get water from the river, and we found a settler had started a ranch at the spring where we expected to stop. His farm, as Fisher explained in disgust, consisted of "five potatoes and a radish." But it was all he had, and he objected to our camping near it, as we had so much stock that he feared it would "endanger his crop," so we continued a mile or two onward and upward into the gorge of the Middle Cañon where we found another spring and camped. This was a work of no little difficulty. The ground was all stone, if the bull may be permitted, and it was almost impossible to get either the tent poles or pins to penetrate into it sufficiently to hold. We had to roll stones around them and brace them in different ways to get them sufficiently anchored to hold the tent up. This was the more difficult as there was a constant breeze through the cañon. The cañon itself was very narrow ; it did not seem to be more than 100 yards across, but it must have been much wider. I tried to ascertain the distance by firing a few shots with my rifle sights adjusted for seven hundred yards, but could not hear the spat of the bullet on the rocks on the other side, or see its impact even with a glass.

The scene was wild and savage in the extreme. On both sides of us rugged mountains, towered almost perpendicularly 3,000 feet above. Through the narrow pass between them, the Yellowstone, swollen by the melting snow from the mountains, tore and plunged like a mad thing. It is the most treacherous of streams, full of whirlpools and eddies, which suck down the strongest swimmers. I had had great expectations of fishing here, but whether it was the swollen stream or not, I was only able to catch two small trout with the fly, and one large one with a grasshopper, although I tried them in the evening and morning, with every variety of lure. It must have been an "off day," as great catches are made by fishermen all along this cañon, many coming up by train from the Mammoth Springs for that purpose.

I found climbing up the lofty banks of this rocky river after fishing to be no easy task. We were now getting to so high an altitude, that the greater rarity of the air was very noticeable. This was particularly the case in climbing, and at first it seemed after making a prolonged exertion, as if we could not inhale air enough.

When Fisher and I, climbing up from the river, had nearly reached the top of the bank, which was not only high, but steep and rocky, we heard a sharp *biz-z-z*, a sound which once heard is never forgotten.

"Rattlesnake!" exclaimed Fisher, hastily picking up a stone. I grasped my fishing rod (which, being unjointed and in its case made quite a respectable club), braced myself as well as the steep bank on which I stood would allow and looked about for the snake. But he had dived into some hole and was gone, at which I must confess, I was extremely glad, as it was a nasty place to have a snake fight. This was the first and only snake I saw or heard during all my trip, although I picked up several discarded skins. While I was fishing, my wife had gone up to the spring and when there she heard the rattle of another snake. At first she thought it was a locust, but when she decided what it was, she could not stay to see him, as she remembered just then she might be needed in camp. She had been so tired from her ride that her climb to the spring had been a slow one. The rapidity with which she descended was extreme, and may perhaps be regarded as another proof of the bracing qualities of the climate. The Park itself has no reptiles, except a few little sand lizards.

The cañon in which we were camped is the resort of

mountain sheep, which find their home in the inacessible
precipices which border upon it. The mountain opposite
our camp was called Sheep Mountain, from the number
of them which resort to it, and the ladies watched its
rugged sides as long as the light would permit in the
hope of seeing some sheep make their appearance upon it,
but were disappointed.

On leaving camp the next morning our way laid over
the private road of "Yankee Jim," a curious character,
of vivid imagination and great flow of language, whom
we had heard spoken of (but doubtless by slanderous
tongues), as "the greatest liar in Montana." Whatever
may be his character as to veracity, Yankee Jim knows
how to build a thoroughfare. He has spent $25,000 in
constructing a toll road twenty-five miles long, three
miles of which is through the gorge of the Middle Cañon,
of the Yellowstone, where the river is compressed by
rocky cliffs, into a space of less than 100 feet, through
which it rushes and tumbles like the rapids of Niagara.

The roadway is a narrow track constructed along the
mountain side, winding up and down projecting spurs,
skirting the edges of high cliffs and overhanging the
tumbling river, in a manner not at all calculated to
soothe the nerves of a poor rider. In some parts we
really trembled for the safety of the wagon, as the wheelers were colts, only a few weeks from the prairie, and a
single shy or bolt of either of them would have sent the
whole outfit over the precipice into the raging torrent
below. Our men, however, were skillful and brought
everything down safely.

I never paid any toll with as much good will as I did
that of Yankee Jim. While his charge was high, I felt
he deserved it for providing a decent passage through
such a rocky gorge, which otherwise would have been
impassable. On the way we met a flock of ruffed grouse
the head of one of which I shot off with my rifle before

THE LOWER CAÑON OF THE YELLOWSTONE.

it took the alarm (a sportsman being allowed to shoot a bird sitting, if he uses a single ball and aims at the head), and after they flew I secured several others with the shot-gun, making a welcome addition to supper, as they were large enough to be good eating, although it was early in the season. The game law might not have been up, but that is understood not to apply when one shoots for food and not for sport. Here as on various other occasions, a good dog would have enabled me to largely add to my bag.

The road was so steep and dangerous that all had to dismount and hold their horses while I was shooting, for fear they might become alarmed at the report of the gun, while the men on the wagon stopped it and blocked its wheels. We found, however, that after the first few shots the horses paid but little attention to the firing.

After passing through this gorge we camped below a railroad bridge, some distance beyond the end of the cañon and close to the Yellowstone, where the fishing was quite good, the trout being plenty although not large.

The following day's ride took us through cañons and plains much like those previously passed over, except that several contained the craters of extinct volcanoes. These were perfect circles, plainly marked, not only by the different color of the grass, but also by a depression below the surrounding soil.

In one or two small ponds had formed, in which ducks were swimming, although it was very early in the season for them.

Later on we passed Cinnabar Mountain and the "Devil's Slide." The mountain is a huge peak which projects sharply into a valley, and derives its name from a broad stripe of cinnabar (a shade of pink), which runs down two of its sides.

The "Slide" consists of two gigantic walls or dykes of

trap rock, each 500 feet wide and 200 feet high, their tops covered with trees, which project out of the side of the mountain, from base to summit. There is a space of some 200 feet between them, making a dark cañon, on each side of which these dykes stand as upright and smooth as if built by human hands. Adjoining them are bands of red and yellow, which make their dark shadows deeper by contrast.

Cinnabar Valley, which extends eight to ten miles beyond this, was emphatically the meanest country encountered during our journey. Level as a floor, baked as hard as a brick by the sun, the soil is so arid that nothing grows naturally upon it, except a little spindling sage brush, interspersed with prickly pear, averaging about one plant to the square foot. The prickly pear is a low spreading plant with broad leaves, the size of the hand, which are covered with thorns, as if a paper of tacks had been emptied on them, all with their business ends up, as I ascertained the first time I sat down on one. It has a pretty flower of all shades, from scarlet to lemon yellow, producing a rich salmon effect. To pick them one needs a pair of tin gloves, as the spines will penetrate a thick driving glove with ease. The valley also rejoiced in possessing a large proportion of alkali in the soil, which made the dust extremely disagreeable. Yet people had settled there, and at one or two ranches, where there was irrigation, we were surprised to see fields bearing quite respectable crops. Hemmed in on every side by high mountains, every breath of air was excluded, while the sun beat into it like a furnace; consequently the ride across it was extremely hot and tiresome. The heat was so great that the ladies got out their umbrellas from the wagon and raised them, but slowly and with great care, for fear of stampeding the ponies, who were not familiar with those refinements. The horses, however, were tired and languid from the heat and paid no attention to them, so they rode forward in comfort. As we reached the end of the valley, where the Park branch of the Northern Pacific terminates, a dashing young ranchman rode out from behind some buildings. He had a spirited horse and rode well, and he knew it. Ladies were scarce in the valley, and the opportunity of displaying his horsemanship and personal graces to two at once was not to be thrown away. So he swung his horse around and rode towards us, making his steed curvet and prance while he swayed to the motion as easily and gracefully as if in an arm-chair. While we were admiring him, a sudden gust of wind came whirling out of a cañon. It caught my daughter's umbrella and instantly turned it inside out, with a loud "crack." At the unwonted sight and sound, our horses, roused from their lethargy, simultaneously reared, snorted and bolted in different directions, and at the top of their speed. The steed of our gallant ranchman was even more frightened than ours. It ran half a mile with him, and as we last saw him he had all he could do to keep it from dashing into a barbed wire fence. The change from his jaunty air to that of anxiety to keep his horse out of that fence was sudden and most ludicrous. I fear his pride had a sad fall.

We could do nothing with the horses until May threw away her umbrella and even then none of our steeds would approach it. As Fisher said, "umbrellas and cayuses don't agree!"

We stopped at Gardner City for dinner. This metropolis consists of two saloons, an eating house, a blacksmith's shop, and as many as eight or ten other buildings. We enjoyed there quite a good dinner, however, (the only meal we took under a roof during our trip) and also obtained a dozen bottles of beer, which I had concluded we needed. Some of the residents gave me a glowing account of the game in the neighborhood, and assured me that on the mountain opposite we could be certain of getting any

STAMPEDED BY AN UMBRELLA.

quantity of mountain sheep. I listened with that incredulous feeling which experience teaches the sportsman to give ear to the flattering narratives of hotel keepers. On repeating the statement to Fisher, he fairly snorted with disgust. "Sheep, indeed," said he; "there hasn't been a sheep on that mountain in five years;" and Fisher was generally right.

While here, we were overtaken by Doctor L——, the Post surgeon from Fort Ellis, with his wife and little boy. The Cheyenne affair had been settled, and he had obtained leave to accompany us. His outfit swelled our party into quite formidable proportions, and his society, and that of his wife, was a most welcome addition to the pleasures of the trip. We also picked up many valuable suggestions from their long experience, one of which was to travel with chickens. Dead chickens have been frequent in most camps with which I have been associated, but this was the first time I had ever seen live ones in that connection. Mrs. L——, however, traveled with a box full. At each camp they would be released, when they would forage for themselves in the grass for bugs and worms, and among the grain dropped by the horses, never going but a short distance from the camp. At night they perched on the wagons, and once or twice under the cot of their fair owner, greatly interfering with her slumbers on these occasions. In the morning they would be caught and re-boxed, usually after quite a lively chase, which afforded considerable amusement to those not engaged in it. Every few days a couple would be killed, and they formed no mean addition to our bill of fare. Our army friends used cots and we tried them for awhile, but finally returned to first principles and the bosom of mother earth. If the ground is stony, damp or infested with anything objectionable in the way of snakes or bugs, a cot is an advantage. But a person is so much colder when sleeping in one than when lying on the ground, that we preferred the latter. We used a thin mattress spread over a buffalo robe, and found the ground always warm and dry. Besides, the slats of an army cot are harder than the nether millstone, the hardest ground being soft in comparison.

For a few miles after leaving Gardner City, we rode through the romantic Cañon of the Gardner, a small but swift stream, whose dancing waters and little cascades, bordered by luxuriant vegetation, were very grateful after the treeless and waterless country which we had left. Then, taking a steep and dusty road, we crossed a small mountain covered by extinct springs, whose remains, half ashes, half limestone, were scattered all over its slopes, and after a sharp descent we found ourselves on the plateau in front of the Mammoth Springs.

CHAPTER VIII.

THE MAMMOTH HOT SPRINGS.

We camped at four o'clock about a mile beyond the hotel at the Springs, at a place pointed out to us by the obliging Government Superintendent, having made twenty miles during the day. He lives in a house perched on the top of a knoll opposite the Mammoth Springs, a mile or so from water, and exposed to the blazing sun in summer and every blast in winter. It was built there in Indian times for the protection of its occupants, like the old castles on the Rhine, and is about as comfortable to live in as one of those would be. By the time the tents were pitched and horses picketed, our party had become rested, and all went down to see the great Springs.

They are utterly unlike anything that we had imagined. The view from the top of the mountain in approaching under the glare of the sun was disappointing, as so many find to be the case with their first view of Niagara. But like that great marvel of nature, the closer they are examined the more they grow upon one, and the more one appreciates their vastness and beauty.

The region of the Springs has an area of five square miles, but the springs as now in operation, actually cover one hundred and seventy acres. The visitor approaching from the front sees before him apparently a huge frozen waterfall, a petrified but larger Niagara, except that instead of being in a single sheet, it is broken into a series of cascades, white as snow in some places, dingy in others, here a reddish yellow, like iron-rust, and there with broad stripes of soft shrimp pink and terra cotta. At the base of this apparent fall rises a cone forty-five feet high

MAMMOTH SPRINGS.

and some twenty feet in diameter, the crater of an extinct geyser, which is known as the "Liberty Cap," close to which is another known as the "Giant's Thumb," both showing marked signs of dilapidation. As you draw nearer to the waterfall it resolves itself into a vast terrace 200 feet high, and some 500 or more wide, composed of limestone which has been slowly deposited by the water from the numerous hot springs which trickle over it here and there in thin sheets, and which are constantly building up and changing its appearance. This deposit when new, is white as lime and quite hard, but after the water has ceased to flow over it, and it becomes exposed to the air, it becomes dingy in color and friable in texture.

As you start to climb up the face of the terrace you experience a succession of surprises. The summit of each little cascade is found to be a beautiful pool, with scalloped edges, indented and fretted like the most beautiful coral. The steaming water in these is as clear as the air and covers the most exquisite formation, beside which, delicate lace seems coarse and tawdry. The colors are simply indescribable. The most delicate pinks and blues, vivid reds and emerald greens rapidly succeed each other. Winding and climbing here and there along the portions of the rock where the hot water from the springs is not flowing, and following the ledges which separate the springs themselves, you finally reach the summit of the first terrace, but not until after many halts, to admire the formations and, what is still more important at that altitude, to regain your breath.

Here is found a broad plateau several acres in extent, interspersed with hot springs of every description, which well gently out of the rock and flow softly from one pool to another until they reach the edge of the terrace, and then trickle from ledge to ledge down to its base. Some of the springs are a hundred feet or more in diameter and quite deep, the largest being seventy-eight feet in depth. Others are much smaller and more shallow. The largest are a beautiful turquoise blue; others are red, brown, green or yellow in hue. The water in them is so clear that the exquisite formations of the sides and bottoms of even the deepest pools are plainly visible; and along their sides, they exhibit the most vivid tints of cream, salmon and pink. The iron springs show striking shades of red. Others with green tints contain arsenic, and those with yellow contain sulphur. The water itself gives the color to the blue pools, and the chemicals the tints of the others. It was noticeable that the latter never mixed, but remained entirely distinct in the same pool. It was also singular to see that the iron floated instead of sinking, forming a reddish crust like scum on the edges. With the exception of the White and the Black Sulphur, none of the springs are stable, but break out each year in different places, without apparent connection with each other.

In looking into the great " White Spring " the bottom is seen to be covered with irregular rounded forms from the size of an orange upwards, and queerly shaped sticks, some the size of one's wrist, and others six inches in diameter, all joined together in a confused mass and all white as milk. They gave the effect as if it was winter and we were looking at objects covered with sleet and ice. Yet the mind, while unconsciously retaining the association, was puzzled by the incongruity existing between it and the steaming water in which they were lying. We were told that these were small stones and grasses which had fallen into the spring from time to time, and upon which the lime which the water carried in solution had been slowly deposited until they had grown to their present dimensions.

All the springs are boiling hot. Their constituents vary largely. Sulphur springs, iron springs, magnesia springs, soda and silicate springs rise and flow within a short distance from each other, with apparently nothing in common but their temperature. The sulphur spring water, for a wonder, is quite agreeable to the taste and is said to be highly medicinal. Several extraordinary cures of rheumatism from its use are narrated. One man, who came there as a cripple, built himself a hut of boughs (which is still standing) close to the springs, and after bathing and drinking the water for a month or two was completely restored to health. He was working as a carpenter at the hotel at the time of our visit. Quite a prominent German physician, who had made a study of of the springs in the Park, said that some of them were most valuable for nervous disorders, mentioning particularly those containing arsenical solutions. He predicted that the Park would eventually become the great *International Nervous Sanatarium.*

It is certain that before many years these springs will be greatly resorted to by invalids. Irrespective of their healing properties, the pure air of this high altitude must prove beneficial, particularly in cases of malaria and nervous prostration. In fact, from my own experience and that of my friends, I am satisfied that there is no tonic like mountain air in such cases, and that many would derive much more benefit from resorting to New Mexico and other similar places in the winter, than in going to such an enervating climate as Florida.

Beyond the first terrace rises a second (which was not visible from below), the summit of which is five hundred feet above the hotel, and six thousand seven hundred feet above the sea level. This terrace, like the one below it, has been slowly built up by the mineral deposits from the flowing springs. So rapidly is lime deposited, that articles immersed for four days in the water from some of the springs become encrusted a sixteenth of an inch. Most visitors arrange to have some trifle, such as a pine cone, fern branch, etc., left in the water until it is coated, to take away as a souvenier; and there is a man at the springs who makes a business of attending to such matters.

The Government keeps a guide at the springs to prevent vandalism, and to avoid accidents to visitors. It is certainly a great consolation to have him precede you as you pick your way along the formation with boiling springs on either hand, and hear others rumbling just beneath you in a way which causes grave doubts as to the solidity of what you are walking on. He was full of statistical and other information, which would be interesting, if I could recall it.

On the second terrace the supply of water seems to be failing. There are a number of beautiful caves full of stalactites of a dazzling white and of extraordinary shapes, left by ancient springs, which have dried up or changed their course. That these changes are frequent, is shown by numbers of trees more or less imbedded in the lime deposits which are scattered about in different places. On the side of the upper terrace is a cave from which issues a gas so deadly that we were told that birds flying within two feet of it would be instantly struck down and killed. Of course, there is a " Lover's Leap " on this terrace. Few of the respectable " wonders of nature " are without something by that name. We were unable to learn why any lover should go to the trouble of a trip to this place, when there were so many more desirable jumps much more convenient. Close to the " Leap " is a petrified geyser which has been split by frost exactly in half. This enables one to clearly trace the way in which it has been built up; the action of the water as it rose higher and higher until it finally reached above the mouth of the tube and was thrown into the air, being clearly apparent by different layers of the deposits, like the rings in the trunk of a tree. So perfect was the representation that as we stood below it we could almost feel as if it was still in action and there was danger that it would fall upon us.

Above the second terrace rises a third, near the summit of which a dark hole suddenly yawns in front of the visitor. A rude ladder projects out of this and leads into a cave below, once occupied by a large geyser. It is now filled with bats, which hang around its roof and darkest recesses in great clusters. When alarmed by the lights of an exploring party, they detach themselves from their roosts and fly clumsily around, until it seems as if the air was alive with them ; their peculiar noise, number and singular shape and flight, as seen by the faint light, producing a most weird effect upon the observer.

These terraces are not the only places where the springs exist. The hillside for fully a mile back is covered by terrace after terrace of extinct springs, until they are gradually lost in the thick woods on the summit of the mountain. There are said to be fourteen of these terraces, which can be clearly traced. The river bank is also lined with many boiling springs, which are still active. Yet immense as these springs seem to be, they are insignificant with what they have been in the past ages, when the Sheep-eater Mountains, and the high crags at Bear Gulch and elsewhere in this neighborhood, were built up by their deposits.

The hotel at Mammoth Springs, the point of departure for all visitors, is a surprising structure for the wilderness. It was built by Rufus Hatch, who is fond of "discounting the future," and is some four hundred feet long, with rooms for three hundred guests, electric lights and other modern improvements. It would do credit to Long Branch. On its broad piazzas were encountered a queer conglomeration of persons. There were travellers from all over the world, averaging at least five foreigners to one American ; for our own people are more eager to see the wonders of foreign lands than those of their own country. Engineers and army officers, railroad men and cowboys, travellers and stage drivers all mingled on a footing of equality. A man's dress gave no clue to his vocation or social position. The wearer of a dilapidated hat, ancient blouse and trowsers showing signs of frequent acquaintance with the saddle, was a U. S. Engineer officer in charge of a construction party. His far better clothed companion was one of his teamsters. The individual with a wide brimmed hat, big boots and fierce aspect was a newly arrived "pilgrim" who could not tell a broncho from a cayuse, and the quiet, gentle spoken man near him was a well known hunter and guide. In short, everybody dressed to suit his own fancy. One young gentleman, holding some scientific position in connection with the Geological Survey, certainly bore off the palm. He was very tall and extremely thin. He wore a broad felt hat, short sack coat and had the seat and crotch of his trowsers re-inforced with white buckskin. As he walked across the piazza the buckskin blended with the color of the limestone, and made him look like a veritable "living skeleton." At the other end of the piazza was a lady dressed in a fashionable silk dress, with a little child dressed to correspond, playing around her.

We were fortunate in finding a number of friends among the army men, and learned from one of the U. S. Engineer officers that the eruptions of great geysers were due on the 22nd. He also very kindly gave his aid in planning our route through the Park to the best advantage, it being important with so much stock as we had, to know the best camping grounds.

CHAPTER IX.

EAST FALLS OF THE GARDNER.

On the 18th our party rode out to the East Falls of the Gardner. The road winds along the side of the Cañon to a rustic bridge thrown across the river just at the head of the Falls. The ascent is gradual and the road good. There is one place where the road goes down a steep hill to within a few feet of the edge of the Cañon and then turns sharply to the left. The ladies were riding in a four-mule ambulance, belonging to Dr. L.'s party, as their faces were still tender. Just at the middle of the hill, the two leading mules, with the perversity of their race, "Jack-knifed," turning short around and walking between the wheelers. The driver put on his brakes and endeavored to turn them by whipping their heads, but without avail. Fortunately I was near and was able to turn them back to their proper positions before any harm was done. If they had become unruly or the brakes had slipped, the chances were excellent that the whole "outfit" would have gone over into the Cañon, and I experienced a few uneasy moments before I got them straightened out, and under the driver's control.

The day was hot, the sun blinding ; and after our long ride over treeless prairies in the glare of the sun, the cool air and luxuriant verdure of this cañon were peculiarly refreshing.

A log bridge extends across the river at a depression in the bank a short distance above the edge of the upper falls. While the men of the party were looking after the horses and getting out the lunch, the ladies went down to the bridge to enjoy the view. My wife and daughter stopped there to rest in the shade and sketch the charming view. Mrs. L. crossed the bridge and, being of a somewhat adventurous disposition, walked out on the slope of the bank above the cañon to take a look at the falls from that point. While the slope was comparatively slight, the bank was covered with pine needles and was very slippery. She had her little boy in her arms to keep him from danger. Suddenly, to her unspeakable horror, her feet lost their hold on the grass and she began to slowly slide towards the edge of the chasm. Embarrassed as she was by the child, she was unable to regain her foothold. The men of the party were out of sight and the noise of the falls rendered unavailing any attempt to call them. My wife caught sight of her at this instant, and at once rushed across the bridge and up the bank. Leaning forward, she reached the handle of her umbrella, which, most fortunately, Mrs. L. was able to seize, and by its aid to scramble into a place of safety.

This was one of the most narrow escapes of the trip. Those who think a woman cannot keep a secret will be surprised to learn that the ladies never mentioned the occurrence during the trip, and I never even heard of it until after we were safely home.

The Gardner appeared to be just suited for trout, and during our return I tried my flies at several points in the stream below the falls where I could clamber down to it. This was far from easy, as the banks were steep and overhung with trees and briars. Perhaps the sun was too bright, or more probably, the stream was so near the hotel as to be "fished out," but I could not even secure a rise.

After returning to camp we again visited the Mammoth Springs and enjoyed its beauties until nightfall and by moonlight. While they appeared beautiful by day, their attractions were increased ten fold by the silvery light of the moon, which brought into strong relief the beautifully fretted and cascade-like formations, and added new colors to the steaming pools. We climbed to the highest point of the upper terrace. Here there was nothing but the crumbling remains of extinct springs and a few petrified trees. A dreary spot in the daytime, it was additionally so as the cold moonlight brought into vivid relief the dark forms of the dead trees and sharply outlined the shadow of their straggling branches upon the white and crumbling deposit like an electric light. Not a sign of life, animal or vegetable, was to be seen, and the stillness was deathlike. Suddenly, with as much dignity as was consistent with his appearance, a huge Jack-rabbit appeared from behind a dead sage brush and hopped out upon the silvery plain. Then catching sight of us he gave an astonished flap of his great ears, and hopped gravely back into the shadows from which he had emerged. He was only a rabbit, but his appearance in the moonlight was startling, and made him seem like some eerie creature from the rumbling depths below us.

CHAPTER X.

THE MIDDLE FALLS OF THE GARDNER.

The 19th being Sunday, the ladies rested in camp, while I took our three men and rode to the Middle Falls of the Gardner. There was no road ; merely a blazed trail through the woods, which we had to hunt up. This involved fording the river and considerable skirmishing among fallen timber, and in and out of places where I would never have dreamed at the East of venturing on horseback. Finally, the trail (probably an old elk runway) was found. It was just wide enough for a horse to get through, and led us up the mountain by a comparatively easy grade, but along a precipice, with yawning depths, to glance into which was sometimes quite startling. But we were rapidly becoming accustomed to that sort of thing and took it as naturally as our ponies did.

After a steady climb of four miles, we found ourselves on the edge of a cañon overlooking the falls. It was a magnificent and most picturesque sight. Mr. Winson's very accurate guide book gives the depth of the cañon at from 1,200 to 1,500 feet. I think this is an error as this would be deeper than the Great Cañon (which the same authority gives at 1,200 feet) and I should think the latter was considerably the deepest. But whatever the measurement, it is of appalling depth, about 500 yards wide at the top and very narrow at the bottom, not to exceed 150 feet. The sides drop from the brink above in almost perpendicular ledges, as steep as the Palisades on the Hudson River and four times their depth. Into this cleft in the rocks, the river plunges in one unbroken fall of over a hundred feet and then continues its fall in a series of cascades to the bottom of the dark chasm. The white fall, the tumbling water, and the dark shadows of the cañon, make a striking picture. After fully enjoying the scene, we amused ourselves by rolling large rocks over the cliff. It was wonderful to see a stone the size of a trunk leap into the air in a plunge of 200 or 300 feet, strike the shelf below as if thrown by a catapult, and with such tremendous force as to rebound twenty feet, and after a series of such terrific bounds, make another tremendous leap to the slope below, continuing in bound after bound until it reached the creek, growing smaller and smaller at each movement until it seemed no larger than a foot-ball.

While indulging in this boyish sport a faint shout came up from below signifying that there was some one down in the cañon. It is unnecessary to say that we at once stopped the stone rolling. Looking down we saw a party of fishermen from the hotel dodging up the bottom of the cañon with great celerity and evident anxiety as to whether any more stones might be expected. So great was the depth, that they looked like children.

While watching them, Horace's hat blew off and lodged in the shelf at the foot of the cliff at the brink of which we were standing. It seemed only a short way down, and we undertook to fasten the picket ropes of the horses together so as to aid him to descend, but found they would not begin to reach the distance. Horace was determined to have his hat, and with regular western recklessness started to climb down. By selecting places where the fragments from the sides of the cañon had formed a slope, and clinging to the trees and shrubs, he managed to work his way to the shelf below, and up on that to his beloved head-gear. He had to go so far down that he appeared only half his natural size. The exploit was more hazardous than we imagined. Mr. Davis, of the Northern Pacific Railroad, as I was afterwards told, undertook to climb up near that very spot only a day or two before. The loose stone slid under his feet, as is common in mountain climbing, but which, though fatiguing, is not dangerous if one keeps moving. Finally, he climbed out on a large boulder, the size of a small house, to look around. Suddenly he discovered that it too was in motion. He slid along upon it for some distance expecting it would roll at every instant, when fortunately, it passed so near a tree that he was enabled to spring into the branches, while the boulder went crashing downwards for a thousand feet, snapping the trees like pipe stems in its course.

After our return the men of the party took a swim in Bath Lake, a beautiful circular pool some 150 feet in diameter, which is just back of the upper terrace of the Mammoth Springs. It has a large hot spring at one end, enabling the bather to select any temperature he may prefer, from tepid to boiling. After our long ride, the warm bath proved most delightful. The water, however, was so strongly impregnated with lime that, as it dried on us upon leaving the water, it made our skin look as if we had been whitewashed and our hair and beards feel harsh. I washed some underclothes in it and they also felt so harsh to the touch as to be uncomfortable.

From the Mammoth Springs to the Norris Geyser Basin is twenty-one miles, and was a journey which we had looked forward to with no pleasant anticipations. Formerly the road was directly over a mountain 3,000 feet high, and was so steep that Fisher had calculated that it would take the wagons the best part of the day to ascend it. It was therefore gratifying to find that the Government engineers had constructed a new road through the cañon of the Gardner, which avoided the mountain altogether and made it possible to cover the distance in a single day.

CHAPTER XI.

GREEN RIVER AND OBSIDAN   CLIFFS.

Breaking camp early we were on the road at half-past seven on the 20th.   Our two days' rest had removed all feelings of fatigue.   The horses were full of life and we loped along briskly.   The road was admirable, like eastern Macadam, and it followed the narrow cañon of the Gardner.   This was so hemmed in by mountains that a shelf had to be blasted out of their sides to support it.   In some places the mountain spurs were so steep and the cañon so deep that trestle-work bridges had been built, which were supported by huge beams set into holes in the rocky precipice.   As we rode along these we were directly over the Gardner, whose swift waters tumbled and tossed in a series of picturesque cascades far below us, giving the effect of the roads in Switzerland which overhang the mountain torrents.   It seemed a " pokerish" kind of a place to drive over, but was perfectly safe.   We had ridden over so many worse places that we did not think so much about it as I have since learned that visitors generally do.   At one place, named the Golden Gate, the rocky face of the mountain is streaked and spotted with rich yellow, which adds greatly to the scene. After riding a mile or more through this gorge, we left the river and turned into the forest.   The effect of this, however, was sadly impaired by the burnt timber which frequently extended along the road for miles and covered the surrounding hills.   Such sights are far too frequent in the Park as is the case in the Adirondacks.   They are caused almost entirely by the carelessness of camping parties.   The Park authorities now have several " fire wardens" patrolling the roads and warning people that leaving a camp-fire burning is punishable by a fine, and it is to be hoped that this will lessen the destruction of the woods and preserve one of the great attractions of the Park.

As we rode through what had once been a thick forest we were astonished at encountering that product of Eastern civilization, a tramp. Blear-eyed and dirty, clothed in a patchwork of rags, with a smoky tin pot at his side, he would have taken the first prize at a tramp show. He sat by the roadside and never condescended to raise his eyes as we rode by. He was the only tramp we saw during our wanderings, and what he was doing in that wild country, or how he lived, was always a mystery to us.

After leaving the cañon the road passes through some small prairies, or parks. As we entered one we saw a coyote slinking over the ridge beyond. I tried to stalk him ; but, as the boys said, he had an engagement and could not wait. He was the only game we saw in the Park. These parks extend along a valley or plateau for several miles. In riding through them the visitor is afforded a fine view of the mountains which surround the valley. Electric Peak, whose summit is fringed with clouds so as to give it the appearance of a volcano ; Sepulchre Mountain, which is covered with what seems to be gigantic graves, and others, are here seen to the best advantage.

After a ride of about twelve miles from the Mammoth Springs, we reached Green river. This is a little stream which runs near the road, and parallel to it for a short distance. The water itself is clear, but the sides and bottom are of a singular metallic green, doubtless due to the presence of arsenic. We should not have noticed this particularly if we had not learned from a gentleman who was making his second visit to the park that, on his previous visit, three years before, his party had camped by this creek and drank its water, and that all of them subsequently became severely ill, and were a long time in recovering. Visitors to the park should be careful not to use the water from any of the brooks or springs unless assured by some one familiar with it that they can do so with safety. All peculiar colored waters had better be left alone.

At a short distance beyond Green River the road skirts the base of the "Obsidan Cliffs."

Here, along the eastern shore of Beaver Lake, for a distance of about a thousand feet, rises a wall-like cliff of black volcanic *glass*, from one hundred and fifty to two hundred and fifty feet in hight. It is bright and glistening, but opaque; something like the glass of a black bottle, except that in places it is streaked with red and yellow. The road along the lake was constructed by building fires upon the blocks of glass, after they had been thrown down by blasting, and when they had become heated, throwing water upon them so as to fracture them. It is said to be the only glass road in the world. The contrast between these high black columns glistenin the sun on the left hand, while on the right were the clear and placid waters of Beaver Lake, interspersed with mossy tufts and the green tops of the many old beaver dams which cross it, was most picturesque.

Strata of this glass crop out at intervals all through the Park, some black, some green with white spots (the true volcanic glass), and some with brownish red streaks. The latter was used for arrow heads by the Sheep-eater Indians, who once inhabited the Parks, and we picked up one of them in one of the cañons.*

On the summit of the divide we turned into a grassy glade, surrounded by fine pines, and halted for lunch at

---

* See remarks on the former inhabitants of the Park at page 139.

LAKE OF THE WOODS.

the edge of a pretty sheet of water, known as the " Lake of the Woods."

After taking a good rest we gave our horses the rein, and dashed over the seven miles between the lake and Norris Basin at full speed, having a lovely ride and completing the twenty-one miles at three o'clock.

CHAPTER XII.

THE NORRIS BASIN.

We camped here, under some trees skirting a meadow at the left side of the road, just across the Norris Fork of the Gibbon River, a rapid, clear and cool stream, which winds and turns through the meadow and looks as if it contained trout, but I was unable to find any in it, although I fished in the cool of the evening, when they should have risen if they were there.

Mrs. Kelly keeps the stage house here, and as we rode by our very hearts were rejoiced at observing a sign of "Fresh Milk for sale." Mrs. Kelly's milk is well known all through the Park, and no one passes her place without testing it. We took all she had, and never was milk more appreciated.

After the camp was pitched, we went down the road to the "Basin." As you come down the road toward it from Mrs. Kelly's, you see on the right hand a valley some half a mile long and a quarter wide, white and utterly barren. In its center a small geyser, the "Constant," I believe, throws up jets of hot water and steam every few minutes, while all over its surface jets of steam are rising, showing the presence of boiling water in various degrees of ebullition. As you descend from the road into this valley, you meet on the side-hill what seems to be the gateway of the infernal regions. On the left hand is a crater or opening in the rock about the size of a large barrel, and black as ink, from which a volume of steam escapes with a roar like a dozen North River steamboats letting off steam at once, fairly shaking the solid rock around it, and giving the idea that if anything should occur to choke up this vent, the whole surrounding rock would be blown into the air. So hot is this steam, that a gun-barrel held in it for a moment becomes too hot to be touched. Some one had thrust a pine bough into the opening. It had become shrivelled and blackened by the heat, and the part of it remaining resembled a snake's head. As this vibrated in the steam it resembled some terrific serpent coming from another world, and about to spring upon us.

A short distance to the right was a "mud pot," some twenty feet in diameter, filled with mud of a pale drab, which was boiling so furiously that its surface was constantly springing up in jets and spray two or three feet high, flickering and twisting like the tongues of flame from a bonfire. The sight was appalling. It seemed as if innumerable demons were struggling beneath it to escape. Certainly nothing I ever saw impressed my imagination so strongly.

The valley itself was covered with coarse sand, as if it had been recently overflown. In fact, Mr. Winsor states that two of the largest vents had no existence in 1875, but had become powerful geysers in 1878. Its whole surface is pitted with holes, large and small, in which hot water bubbles and growls, grunts and roars in every tone of the gamut. Some of the pools are black, others white, and others yellow with sulphur. A choice variety of odors is also observable.

Many of the "pools" and "pots" are beautiful. The "Emerald pool," which is on the bank above the valley, is like a fairy's dream. Imagine an almost circular pool some fifty feet in diameter, of the most beautiful emerald tinge, so clear that you can see distinctly the sides and bottom at a depth of twenty feet, while apparently growing all through it are irregular but exquisite formations like large masses of white coral, which glimmer and shine through the green water with an indescribable softness and beauty. It looked like the grottos in which fable tells us the sea nymphs live. Inasmuch as it is boiling hot, they would, however, probably object to this as a residence, notwithstanding its beauty.

On the east side of the main road are several curious "paint pots." One of these is like a pool of white lead twenty feet across. Others are interesting from their brilliant hues. Pink, salmon, red and yellow ; almost every tinge of color is represented.

The ladies made quite a palette of colors by putting dabs of mud from the different pots upon a piece of wood. But like the specimens they obtained from the Mammoth Spring, they crumbled and faded when dried. In this neighborhood hot and cool pools lay side by side, presenting the most astonishing contrast. Why one stream of water should be boiling while another two feet from it is cold, is difficult to explain.

Some vandal hand had wedged a tree trunk into the " Minute Man," and it had retired from active business. At least it did not exhibit during the twenty minutes we waited for it. The " Mammoth " made a fine display, throwing off three heavy jets of boiling water and steam.

The geysers here impressed us greatly, being the first we had seen. They became insignificant afterwards, however, when compared with the great geysers of the Upper Basin, a fact which makes it wise to commence one's tour from the Mammoth Springs.

We were reminded that night that we had reached a high altitude. It was as cold as Greenland. Ice formed in the water pails, and a heavy frost covered the grass. The aspect of the mules in the morning was ludicrous as they stood motionlesss amid the frost-covered grass, with their backs humped up and their heads down, the picture of discomfort and disgust.

But the sun came out bright and warm, and under its rays the mules brightened up, shook off their stiffness and began to graze with the usual aspect of injured meekness, characteristic of those animals.

This meekness, however, was deceptive. Their coolness struck inward, so as to sour their tempers and loosen their heels, and it was the part of wisdom to approach them on such a morning carefully and from the front end only.

CHAPTER XIII.

GIBBON CAÑON AND FALLS.

Time would not permit a visit to the "Gibbon Paint Pot Basin," or the "Mammoth Geyser Basin." Both are some distance off the road and are only reached by a trail through the woods. The former contains five hundred mud and boiling springs of every imaginable color, and is said to be well worth a visit. The latter is a basin of some five acres and is full of hot springs and the remains of extinct geysers. After a ride of a few miles from camp we reached the Gibbon Cañon, a chasm where there was scarcely room for the road between the rushing river and the base of the cliffs. The latter tower upward perpendicularly for 2,000 feet, so that a stone falling from their summit would apparently have fallen upon us. Although the sun was high, it was cool in the cañon, and the luxuriant foliage, the sparkling river, and the dark and frowning over-hanging rocks made a most striking scene.

Emerging from the pleasant shade and cool air of the Cañon we rode for several miles through a forest of "bull pine," (bastard fir) the predominant timber in the Park. These are caricatures upon the true pine, tall and slender like small telegraph poles, and growing so closely that a horse cannot pass among them. Yet, strange to say, in a forest of this kind, where the trunks of the trees are so close that the eye cannot penetrate a hundred feet, there is little more actual shade than upon a treeless prairie. The few needles they have for leaves hang limp and apparently wilted, interposing no barrier to the sun's rays, while the trunks are too small to afford any protection, to the great disgust of the weary traveler.

As the sun climbed higher, it grew hotter, so that it was difficult to believe that it had been so cold the night before. The trees kept off the wind, while affording no shade and the road was dusty. In the openings we would catch a breeze which was most enjoyable, but it was far from being comfortable in the woods.

About seven miles from camp we reached the falls of the Gibbon, and tying our horses to the trees we climbed down the side of the cañon. It was a pretty severe climb, down an almost perpendicular cliff, and the Government engineers might expend some labor there to advantage. The sight, however, more than repaid the trouble. The river glides over a rocky shelf and falls in a plunge of full eighty feet, dividing into two sheets, one being an unbroken torrent, and the other a thin sheet resembling a huge veil of delicate lace, constantly broken and re-produced.

I returned up the bank a few minutes before the others to look after the horses. As I stood there a stage drove by full of passengers, among whom was the familiar face of a New York lawyer, and it was amusing to see his look of curiosity at the *outré* figure, with yellow helmet, gray clothes and leggins, all plentifully covered with dust, change into the recognition of a familiar face.

A few miles further on I was still more surprised to meet a stage containing another friend, a lawyer from Albany, who was returning from the Grand Geysers and Great Cañon, and declared with emphasis "that there was nothing like them in the world," an opinion in which I found that he was perfectly correct. At the Geysers I met still another New York lawyer, showing that the members of that profession with their usual sagacity know what portions of the country were worth visiting. These gentlemen, like most of those that we met in the

FALLS OF THE GIBBON.

Park, had no more equipment than is usual in traveling, (except that they wore their winter clothing) and needed no more.

Fording the warm waters of Cañon Creek we rode for about a mile along almost the only bad road we met in the Park. It was a new road, and a large gang of men were at work upon it. Not having had time to harden, it was extremely dusty and made hard pulling for the teams.

From here onward we rode over a succession of fir clad terraces, "the charms of which (as the Guide Book says) are apt to cloy." We found them extremely monotonous, particularly upon a hot day. I have since been informed that a new road has been constructed, which is now used as a substitute for this one, and which avoids some of its disagreeable features.

While jogging along, our attention was attracted by vociferous singing in the rear. "Can these be cowboys on a spree?" one of the ladies anxiously asked. Soon there emerged from a dust cloud a four-horse stage, laden with a full cargo of clerical gentlemen, of no particular denomination, but smooth shaven and stout, who apparently were not paying the slightest attention to the scenery, but were making the woods fairly rattle with Sunday-school hymns, the melody being occasionally broken by the cries of their driver to his horses. Our pace was about the same as theirs; and for a full hour we could hear them roll out a steady stream of song, which echoed and re-echoed at times from the mountains with startling effect.

While Fisher and I were about to drink from a little creek, a buckboard drove up with two men whom Fisher knew. They produced a bottle of "cordial" and invited us to "smile," and I then had the honor of an introduction to the County Sheriff. It seemed that a murder had been committed in one of the towns adjoining, and he was after the criminal, who was reported to be hiding with one of the gangs of laborers in the Park.

"He is a red-headed fellow about my size, Fisher; wears boots with big nails. If you see him you bring him in; there's a hundred dollars reward," said the sheriff. "All right, I will," said Fisher.

I inquired if this informal method of appointing a deputy to make arrests was the usual way, and whether such a trifle as a warrant was required? "This is the way we always do it," was the reply.

"But he will show fight, won't he?"

"Oh, yes—but I will fix it so he won't have any chance—catch him off his guard and make him hold up his hands."

It must not be thought, however, that there was anything of the desperado about the sheriff or his deputy. He was a quiet, gentlemanly man, wearing a linen duster, and looking like an ordinary farmer. Although he asked us to drink, it was done as a mere matter of politeness, for none of us took more than a taste. In fact, all the whiskey that was used by our entire outfit, consisting of four men and an occasional visitor, in nearly a month, was one gallon and a half.

At about four o'clock we finished our ride of seventeen miles, and went into camp at Firehole River about four o'clock.

CHAPTER XIV.

FORKS OF THE FIREHOLE RIVER.

At the forks of the Firehole, two of the roads to the principal attractions of the Park converge. Here, also, the road enters which connects with the Central Pacific via Salt Lake City and Beaver Cañon.

There is quite a fair hotel here which is used as a stage station, and also a store at which canned provisions and other supplies needed by camping parties can be obtained. The prices are higher than in Bozeman, seventy-five cents a can for peaches, twenty-five cents for a cigar, etc. Still they have to be transported a long distance, and the season for sales is short.

The river is a still but swift stream, a hundred feet or so in width. Its source is in the Geysers and in the hot springs along its bank ; consequently it is as warm as an ordinary warm bath. It is without fish, but I seldom have enjoyed a bath more than I did the one I took in it ; a warm bath in a swift stream was a new experience and removed the fatigues of the saddle, like a Turkish bath.

The level valley is covered with a coarse growth of grass and is treeless, greatly resembling a large salt marsh. Passing the hotel, we went into camp half a mile further up the river, at a place where President Arthur and his party had camped during the recent visit of the former, and near to where a cool spring comes out of the river bank. It is one of the peculiar features of this country, that there is not the slightest connection between directly adjoining springs. If one is boiling, the next may be cold. An iron spring adjoins a sulphur one, and an alum spring is side by side with a lime spring; as if they were conducted in pipes from distant reservoirs.

Here I may say that we found the reports about the unfitness of the water in the Park for drinking, to be largely moonshine. Cold springs, such as one meets in the Adirondacks are comparatively rare, and at some places the water is unpleasantly warm, and in a few others full of alum, sulphur and other chemicals. But we were always able to manage our marches so as not to camp at any place where the water was not drinkable. We drank a great deal of beer, it is true, but we could have got along reasonably well without it. It was of the most value at lunch, as it permitted us to stop when water was not to be had.

While pitching camp, the old Fire Warden, quite a striking looking man, with long beard and broad brimmed hat, mounted on a tall broncho, and having a tin can slung at his pommel, rode up to warn us about extinguishing our camp fires. He informed us that the " Fountain " Geyser would " go off " at 5 P. M.. so we at once mounted and rode out to see it. The road crossed the river, passing a log-house with open grated door, built for a jail for violators of the Park laws, around which some little children were playing. We then left it and rode along the west side of the marsh. Presently, the grass disappeared and the geological formation changed to a peculiar gravelly rock, found in the geyser district, which rose with a gentle slope into a sort of mound, interspersed here and there with shallow rills and pools of hot water.

Although our horses had walked through the Norris Basin with the utmost courage, yet, we had doubts as to whether they might not be as frightened at a first-class geyser as at an umbrella. There being too much hot water about to make it safe to manage a frightened horse, we left our steeds at some distance from the geyser and proceeded on foot, leaping over the small streams of hot water, and giving the pools a wide berth.

The "Fountain" has no elevated crater, but springs from a basin in the centre of this mound. This is almost circular and is some fifty feet in diameter. Its sides slope inward with peculiar rounded lumps, like rocky cushions, which is quite characteristic of the geysers. This basin was brim full of furiously boiling water. From time to time the latter would be thrown violently upward at several different places, and dashed and tossed about until the whole surface was converted into a mass of foam, and then the disturbance would as suddenly subside. As we gazed, these foaming centres grew larger and more turbulent, and their intervals of subsidence became more brief. Finally, with a great roar, they all united in a solid mass of boiling, foaming spray and steam, which enveloped the whole pool and shot upward to a height of twenty-five feet. This remained in position for a short time, faltered, dropped, and again shot upward for several minutes. Then it stopped, gurgled and groaned, and the water sunk and disappeared, leaving the pool quite dry, and an empty orifice at one end some twenty-five feet deep, the tube of the geyser. Usually the column rises at least fifty feet high. Compared with the great geysers we saw afterward, the sight was not remarkable, but to novices, as we then were, it was thrilling enough.

A short distance from the "Fountain" is the "Jet" Geyser, a pool of some twenty feet in diameter. It works apparently under difficulties, for when in action, the earth around trembles and throbs, the water boils and is dashed violently in all directions, while a jet shoots up in the centre to a height of about fifteen feet.

Separated by a line of trees from these geysers, is the curious freak of nature called the "Mud Caldron." It is a pool of about forty by sixty feet, filled with boiling white mud, that looks like white lead, or plaster of Paris. It does not boil violently, but simmers peacefully, while all over its surface bubbles of steam constantly form and break with a curious *blob blob*. It has a sickly yet sinister look, reminding one of the "shivering sands" that Wilkie Collins describes in the Moonstone.

At one end of this basin are found some thirty or forty small craters or mud pots of the most delicate shades of pink and rose, and which are really beautiful.

Not far from these are the "Thud Springs." They are of a peculiar dark-green color, and a constant stream of steam escapes through them from some vast subterranean fountain, with a force which shakes the ground and makes a muffled "*thud*"—"*thud*," which sounds something like the escape of steam from a locomotive, and is quite trying to the nerves.

All around these wonders for a distance of several miles are a number of other mud pots, boiling springs and small geysers, to enumerate which would be tedious, but which are well worth an examination.

After our return to the camp, two of the ladies drove up to the hotel and purchased some steak for a change of diet. When they came back, they reported that one of them had seen a "red-headed man" hanging about the hotel. The question at once was whether or not it was the one that Fisher was to arrest. It was amusing to see how the man-hunting instinct of the savage, which lies so close to the veneering of civilization on which we all plume ourselves, began to break out.

We were none of us officials, and were under no obligation to hunt up a criminal. If we got him, the result would be a delay which would disarrange and perhaps break up our trip ; and, in addition, the getting him was likely to be quite a serious affair. Our men, however, thought nothing of all this, but were wild to get down to the hotel, and in a few minutes were off with all the revolvers in camp in their pockets.

Dr. L. and I moralized for some time about the foolishness of their conduct, and then thought we would drive down ourselves, not of course to mingle in the difficulty, if there should be any, but purely as spectators. I was just putting my Winchester in the Doctor's buggy (thinking that I could perform the part of a spectator to more satisfaction if it was handy), when the men came back in extreme disgust. It was a red-headed man, but not the right one. *He* had gone off into some of the mining camps around the Park several days ago. And then Fisher moralized how embarrassing it would have been to have captured him, and how glad he was that he was not there.

At night we were reminded that we were 7,236 feet above the sea, by a heavy frost and ice in our water pails ; but we had plenty of blankets and had no trouble in keeping comfortable.

The 22nd found us early in the saddle, for the eruption of the great Geysers was announced for the next day. Passing over the marsh which contains the "Fountain," and crossing a number of small but hot brooks, which our ponies sniffed at with supreme contempt and crossed with caution, we kept along the valley of the Firehole, which soon became narrow, and enclosed with high hills.

CHAPTER XV.

THE GREAT GEYSERS.

After riding about five miles, a cloud of steam on the opposite side of the river announced our arrival at what the guide book terms "Egeria Springs," but which is popularly known as "Hell's Half Acre." Fording the rapid and stony Firehole, our ponies clambered up the rocky bank on the other side, and after tying them to some trees, a few steps brought us to the edge of the "Excelsior," the largest geyser in the world. This is emphatically "a terror," if the expression may be permitted.

Imagine a pit like a huge cellar, two hundred and fifty feet in diameter, sunk fifteen to twenty feet deep in the solid rock and full of water, boiling and seething like the most gigantic caldron conceivable, while from the whole surface a column of steam is constantly ascending high in air and almost concealing the water below.

On the river side half the rocky bank has been swept away by some terrific eruption, and through the gap thus formed a stream of boiling water the size of a brook rushes into the river. The other banks overhang the basin and seem tottering to their fall. As one of the men remarked, "It looks as if the whole business might go up at any minute, and if it does so when we are here, it will be a case of ' *Good-bye, John.*' "

The eruptions of the "Excelsior" are rare. I could learn of but two men who had actually seen one. These reported that the column was sixty feet in diameter and ascended three hundred feet ; the volume of water was so great as to sweep away all the bridges over the Fire-hole river; the roar sounded like an earthquake, and huge stones were scattered all over the neighborhood. On the other hand, a good deal of incredulity was expressed on the subject by men who ought to know the truth. The remark of one of this class, a stage driver, sums up their version.

"I have heard," said he, "lots of stories about the 'Excelsior' a guisen, from men who have heard somebody else tell about it. But I a'int seen no one who has seen it with his own eyes, and I don't expect to. In my opinion, it never did guise and it a'int never agoin' to."

This was the first time I ever heard the verb "to guise," but it struck me as quite appropriate.

Language fails me to fitly describe the beauty of the "Grand Prismatic Spring," which adjoins this geyser. General Terry expressed to me the opinion that this was the most beautiful thing in the Park. Its dimensions are immense (two hundred and fifty by three hundred feet). Although hot, its surface is placid. The colors are indescribable. In the center it is of the deepest, darkest blue, which softly shades off near the edges into a beautiful green. Closer to the shore the tints change into yellow, then to orange, then to dark red, brown, and yellow on a white ground. These colors are formed apparently by the different deposits under the water, and all are strikingly vivid and distinct.

As the steam which rises slowly from it is blown here and there by the wind, the surface is exposed first in one place and then in another, and the eye falls in succession upon color after color, so strangely contrasted, so vivid and yet so beautiful, as they glisten in the bright sunshine, that it seems more like magic than anything which really exists in nature.

To the north is another spring called the "Turquoise," which is a hundred feet square, and a perfect turquoise blue. This would be beautiful elsewhere, but fades into insignificance when compared with the glories of its prismatic neighbor.

The outlets from these springs are almost as beautiful as the springs themselves. As the " Prismatic " softly pulsates, it sends a gentle flow of water over its beautifully scalloped edges, which gathers into pools of softly variagated colors, while the " Turquoise " emits a small meandering stream through various channels of white, salmon color, and yellow.

From here onward, the road wound among and over wooded knolls, making the ride very pleasant. The distance to camp was short, we were all in high spirits, and kept our ponies on the " lope " most of the way. As we neared the Upper Geyser Basin, hot springs became more and more frequent. At Rabbit Branch a boiling stream poured into the Firehole River, and from there to the Geysers rills of hot water and jets of steam seemed to line its banks in endless succession. Nor was this confined to the river side, for on either hand, and far distant amid the surrounding forest, could be seen other columns of vapor, indicating the presence of hot water in various shapes. The name of Firehole is well bestowed upon this valley and river.

On emerging from a clump of trees, the Upper Geyser Basin lay before us. It is a valley about four miles square. The river traverses its center, and the principal geysers are situated within half a mile, on either hand, so that they are strung along in a parallelogram, about three miles long by one wide, within which area four hundred and forty geysers and hot springs are said to have been counted. The valley may be termed level, although it is interspersed with small mounds and knolls on the summit of which the various geysers are situated, and which have been probably built up by their action. With the exception of a few patches of marsh grass and a little scattered timber, the valley is a barren and arid expanse of rough limestone, resembling coarse coral. It is hemmed in on every side by high mountains covered by forests. Throughout its whole extent huge columns of steam are constantly ascending high in air, and in one part of it or another some kind of an eruption is constantly taking place. In walking through it, holes and large pools (the relics of ancient and inactive geysers) are met every few feet, from which mysterious, gurgling, gasping noises are heard, and which render it necessary to take heed of one's steps.

Some of the geysers "go off" or guise (to borrow the driver's expression) every few minutes, some every hour, and some at intervals of several days. As a rule, the larger they are the more time elapses between their eruptions. Some are very regular. "Old Faithful," in particular, does not vary five minutes from an even hour between its performances. The others are not so punctual, and many persons think are growing less so. Certainly the careful table prepared by Mr. Winsor from actual observation is no longer accurate, and even the hotel people were quite mistaken in some of their predictions as to the larger geysers.

A new hotel of the Queen Anne type, (which by the by has been plastered with lime from some of the "paint pots" in the vicinity) fronts directly opposite "Old Faithful," and from its piazza a good view of the entire valley can be obtained. The scene is also enlivened by a long row of tents near the hotel belonging to the Park Improvement Company, and to the Government Surveyors.

Just as we reached the valley, the "Grotto" was obliging enough to "go off" while we were riding quite close to it. Its performance was thrilling, as it threw out huge jets from its various orifices, but our enjoyment was a little dampened by our uncertainty as to what would be

"OLD FAITHFUL."

the effect upon our horses. To our surprise, however, they gave no signs of fright, and acted as if familiar with geysers in eruption from their youth upward.

Passing the "Grotto" and the craters of "Young Faithful," the "Giant," and several other large geysers, we rode to a projecting grove of trees near the center of the valley, and not far from the hotel and went into camp, the situation commanding a view of the whole valley.

While the tents were being pitched and the horses picketed, we walked down to "Old Faithful," which was then nearly due.

A gentle ascent, broken into low steps or terraces over which little streams of water were meandering and forming shallow pools here and there, is crowned with an irregular mass of rock some six feet high and twenty feet in diameter, in the center of which is a hole the size of a hogshead. All around is barren rock of a whitish gray and rough, like a nutmeg grater. The little pools formed in it by the geyser water are of brilliant colors and full of beautiful formations like frost work. As a friend of mine said, "they were like an emerald-tinted stream, flowing in a trough of gold." The crater itself is composed of globular masses of a peculiar rounded appearance, like huge beaded cushions.

While we waited (being careful to keep on the windward side) the crater filled up with hot water, which boiled and tossed and churned itself into foam and then sank away again, then with a gasp and a subdued growl the water shot up two or three feet, and fell back, but not quite so far and again tossed itself into foam. Another louder rumble, and it went up a foot higher than before and fell back again ; then another still louder and the height of six feet was attained, then, just as the water was apparently subsiding, came a tremendous and appalling roar and a mass of seething, scalding water, the entire diameter of the crater, shot bodily up, and up, and

up, in jet after jet until a solid column was created one
hundred and thirty feet high, (which is just about the
height of the Equitable Building in Broadway) and which
gracefully waved in the wind and fell like a cataract opposite us, while the steam rising from it seemed to reach
the very heavens.

No language can depict the grandeur of the sight. At
the first roar we all retreated precipitately to a safe distance. But seeing the regularity of the movement of
the water, we gradually approached to within twenty feet.
After playing about four minutes, the column wavered
and gradually fell, and then with a great gurgle the water
disappeared down the tube of the crater, leaving the latter perfectly empty, but so hot that all traces of water
instantly disappeared. We tried to look over the edge
and to peer into the depths below, but the stones were too
hot to touch, and the steam which came up from the crater could not be breathed. While the water from these
geysers contain far less lime and other materials in solution than that of the Mammoth Springs, it still contains
some. With one exception all the craters of the Great
Geysers are situated on little knolls raised some distance
above the rock surrounding them, which must have been
built up by the water. Many persons write their names
in the little pools, through which the water ejected from
" Old Faithful " finds its way, but no names over two
years old were legible, the others have been gradually
covered by the deposit from the water.

It is quite common for visitors to throw articles of
clothing into this geyser to be washed ; they all come out
in the course of time, but usually in fragments. We
picked up a piece of a silk handkerchief, the size of a finger nail and some similar pieces of flannel shirts. They
were very clean, but their usefulness as clothing was
greatly impaired. One geyser known as the " Laundress,"
is quite celebrated as a washerwoman. It has no erup-

tions, but sends out a steady flow of hot water which is very soft and well suited for cleansing. Our men threw two of the saddle blankets into it. The dirt at once discolored the pool, and when it cleared the blankets had gone. Twenty-fours hours later a corner of one came into sight from out of the geyser tube. Our men got a couple of poles, and by pushing and pulling, managed after a long time to extricate first one and then the other blanket, being nearly parboiled in the operation. The geyser seemed to be screw-shaped, so that the blankets caught in it, and there was frequently a downward suction. The blankets were a good deal torn when they came out, but they were very clean !

The soldiers and servants accompanying our friends from Fort Ellis washed a number of clothes in a hot spring by tying them into a bundle with a picket rope and sousing them up and down, being very careful not to let them get too deep. This worked admirably. One of the girls washed an old cashmere dress and made it look like new. Sam declared that he knew of a party who used to throw their potatoes they wished cooked into a boiling pool which is near the base of the "Castle Geyser," and that when they were cooked they would rise to the surface so they could be fished out !

As we returned to camp we saw a fine eruption from the "Castle Geyser," a pile of rock some twenty feet high, resembling a ruined castle. It has several vents, and while it does not eject the water to as great height as some of the others, it sends out a large volume to the height of from thirty to forty feet, which falls with a heavy splash all around and is accompanied with a tremendous rush of steam which fairly shakes the surrounding earth. Occasionally it shoots up to the height of over a hundred feet, and it has small displays every few hours. Near to it is a beautiful spring, transparent and of a lovely blue, its walls lined with dazzling white.

Not far distant was the "Morning Glory," another pool fully twenty feet across and fifty deep, growing smaller and smaller as it deepened, and exactly resembling the flower from which it was named. The water of a superb blue, was lightest around the edges and the shading towards the center was exquisite.

A sullen roar across the river attracted our attention to a heavy column of water and steam arising from the other side of the river. The "Lioness" was in full blast.

In a short time off went the "Oblong," very much as the "Castle" had done. Every few minutes a little geyser opposite our camp, but on the other side of the river, called the "Saw Mill," would apparently get itself into a frantic state of excitement, sending up a small but beautiful jet of water with a noise like a saw mill in active business.

The glare of the sun on the white formations which surround the geysers was quite trying to the eyes, and after walking over it for a short time watching several of the geysers, we were content to retire into such shade as we could find and observe the others from a distance. As soon as the sun went down we wandered down the valley, climbing up the craters of such of the geysers as were quiet and not too hot, and timing our visit so as to be close to "Old Faithful" at the appointed hour. It was on time as usual, and made a magnificent exhibition. While each geyser has its peculiarities, "Old Faithful" is the most interesting. Its eruptions are certain, almost to the minute; and although some others throw the water they eject to a much greater height, yet, the sight presented by its magnificent column rearing itself majestically upward and then gracefully waving in the breeze, cannot well be surpassed. The clump of geysers known as the "Lion," the "Lioness and Cubs" are close together and derive their name from the growling noise which they emit even when not in a state of eruption. We were told that an Englishman who was visiting the park shortly before our arrival, had sat down on the crater of one of the "Cubs" to wait for the eruption of the "Lioness" and fell asleep. Unfortunately the "Cub" went off before the "Lioness" and he was severely burned before he woke up and got out of the way.

We now came near experiencing a serious misfortune. My wife's saddle was an old one and had been sent to a saddler to be put in order before leaving Bozeman. The man had been careless and had not observed that a strap of iron which had been fastened under the pommel to strengthen it was loose. Our last day's ride had been quite fast, and in riding down some of the hills this iron had become broken and one end of it had cut her pony's back so deeply that it went against our consciences to ride him. "Old Riley," which was the name of the injured horse, had been quite unlucky. He was a white cayuse, with only one eye, but of amiable disposition and easy gait. Early in our trip he had undertaken to roll while picketed and had managed to strike a broken bottle, or something of that description, which had made a long cut in his cheek, which, although not interfering with his usefulness, had detracted largely from his personal appearance. By washing and putting vasaline on it, this cut was doing well when this last accident occurred. This latter occasioned us much annoyance, for it was clear that it would be some time before it would do to put a saddle on him, and although at present my wife could ride either in the ambulance or on the extra mule of our army friends, yet they would soon leave us and unless another horse could be procured we would then be in a bad way. Fortunately, we met the owner of the horse a few days afterwards, he having come on from Bozeman with another party, and obtained from him a new horse in place of poor Riley. With another saddle which Dr. L. loaned us we thus escaped from a great dilemma. It would have been most disagreeable if one of the ladies had been obliged to ride in the wagon, and yet this would have to be done if no other horse could have been obtained. There is nothing which is harder upon a horse's back than a side-saddle. Any one starting off with ladies upon a trip of any length should therefore personally examine the backs of the horses intended for their use and reject all which show marks of saddle galls. He should also be sure that the side saddles are in good order, strong, and that they fit the horses. Fisher told us that the ladies of some parties that he had conducted rode Indian fashion (astride) and that it was much easier upon the horses, and no harder upon their riders.

With a light wagon it would not have been very disagreeable if one of the ladies had been obliged to ride in it, but with our heavy "dead ex" affair it would have been far from pleasant, although the ladies insisted upon proceeding in this way rather than shorten the trip. The new horse, having been used in harness, had a much harder gait than his predecessor, and his "lope" was something which went beyond anything any of us had ever experienced. My daughter voluntered to break him in, claiming that having been accustomed to riding the farm horses she could stand ary gait, but she had to abandon the idea. But he was the best walker I ever saw. He would walk four miles an hour all day ; and however the other horses might lope off he was certain to overtake them before long and compel them to do their best to keep up with him.

We remained in camp on the 23d to see the eruption of as many of the great geysers as possible, particularly the "Grand." This was on the side of the river opposite our camp and close to the hillside. Near it is a small geyser called the "Turban." When this fills up and begins to work actively it is an indication that the "Grand" is getting ready for business. It was now pounding away and the "Grand" was overdue.

The geysers in this basin (except the "Grand") differ from the others we had seen in having regular craters, or cones, composed of rough rock, of varied shapes and rising from three to twenty feet above the ground. The "Turban," however, is an exception, its crater being sunk, so that if a man stood in it, his head would be below the surface of the ground.

Several times during that night we heard the roar and heavy splash of the "Castle," which was within one hundred yards of our camp, as well as the roar of some of the other geysers. But we were too tired to get up to see them; and besides there were too many holes full of boiling water in the neighborhood, to make walking in the night-time attractive.

Early in the morning, fancying I heard the roar of the eruption of the "Grand," I stepped out of the tent and looked around. The sight presented was most impressive. The air was quite cold and still, the light, dim and weird and the steam from all the different geysers and pools formed columns much larger and more distinct than was the case during the daytime.

Throughout the area of the valley, a space of nearly four miles square, and as far as the eye could reach in the dim light there was hardly a space from which a misty column, white and spectral, was not slowly rising and mounting until it seemed to meet the skies. These white and mysterious columns with their steady, upward movement appeared in the gray light of early dawn like an army of spirits assembling; and gave one a most vivid idea of the Judgment Day, "when the trumpet shall sound and the dead shall be raised."

We spent that day roaming over the valley, examining the various geyser craters and springs, and watching their eruptions and in lying in camp, watching and sketching the curious scene, and in getting up our washing.

During our stay a number of stages full of tourists,

ladies and gentlemen, (some of whom we knew) arrived and departed ; but the majority of them, like most travelers, were in too great a hurry to spare the time to see much of anything.

During the latter part of the day the "Splendid" fairly outdid itself, though some credit must be given to the " Comet," a small jet geyser a few feet distant from the "Splendid," that "went off " simultaneously with the latter. The "Splendid" sends a superb column, as high, or higher, than " Old Faithful," but more like spray. This time as both " Comet" and " Splendid " rose into the air, a magnificent rainbow was formed from their spray, that lasted until they wavered and fell back and gave a last touch of beauty to the scene.

We expected the " Grand," " Giant," " Giantess " and " Bee Hive" to go, but they did not do so, although they displayed all the symptoms. I am inclined, however, to think that the eruption of some of them took place during the night, as there was a great noise from somewhere.

Among the objects of interest we saw, were the " Devil's Punch Bowl" and the "Black Sand Basin." The former is a large and beautiful boiling spring with a crested rim extending above the surrounding rock. Its exterior was exactly that of an inverted punch bowl, and its colors were simply dazzling. The boiling water it contained was of an intense blue, while the crested rim shaded from the darkest iron-red to the deepest orange. The bowl, itself was colored by the various chemicals contained in the water in all the tones of terra cotta, shrimp pink and yellow, fading into a white ground, while at the base of the bowl itself were two large pools of green water, deriving their color from arsenic.

The latter was a deep spring of beautiful blue, surrounded on three sides by banks of black sand ten feet high; the water trickles out at the fourth side and through a channel full of variegated yellows and browns, the contrast between the blue water and black sand being very striking.

Night came without the expected eruption of the "Grand" having occurred, and as we were obliged to leave in the morning, we went to bed disappointed. Just at daybreak the cry went through the camp, "Turn out," "turn out, the 'Grand' is going."

Then there was indeed a scurry from our camp and from one or two adjoining. Everybody scrambled to their feet, struggled into the first available garments and ran down the bank of the river, across the little foot-bridge and up the slope beyond at the top of their speed, buttoning as they ran and all filled with great excitement, for the "Grand" was at last in full operation.

Some were wrapped in blankets, others in shawls, or overcoats, some were in their shirt-sleeves and several hatless. But everything was forgotten in the magnificent sight before us.

Although the geyser tube of the "Grand" is small, not over four feet in diameter, its eruption seemed to spread so as take in the whole diameter of the pool, making a column fully fifteen feet in diameter. This enormous mass of water, far larger than we had yet seen, shot straight upward to the height of two hundred and thirty feet (or more than two-thirds the height of Trinity Church steeple) accompanied with tremendous billowy clouds of steam which mounted to double that height, and which, as they were condensed into spray fell all around in a drizzling rain. The rumbling and roaring of the escaping steam and water were terrific. The column seemed to maintain its height by a series of jets, which appeared to be constantly forced up through the central mass. After spouting with great vigor for some five or six minutes, it faltered and subsided. But the water had scarcely attained its original level when it was thrown upward to its previous height with even greater fury and volume than before. We counted seven distinct eruptions, occupying altogether over half an hour. While they were going on, the "Turban" was also in full operation, sometimes throwing the water it ejected into the basin of the "Grand."

Finally, the water in both geysers sank out of sight in their tubes with a loud gurgle, leaving them perfectly empty and so hot that their rocky interior dried instantly.

While we were watching this sublime and awe-inspiring sight, and which in itself was sufficient reward for our whole journey, the wind veered several times. We lost no time in shifting our positions to conform to its direction, for the fall of the water to leeward would have swept a person away like a feather, besides scalding him to death.

Not until the display was over, did we become for the first time aware of our motley apparel ; and then all had a good laugh over each other's ludicrous appearance.

The "Grand" had fully satisfied us, and we broke camp immediately after breakfast, and by six o'clock were again *en route*. Before taking leave of the geysers, it may not be out of place to give an explanation of the causes that are supposed to cause their eruption. Professor Bunsen, who made a special study of the phenomena of the geysers in Iceland, is of the opinion that the tube and mound of a geyser are gradually built by the silica which the water holds in solution. That for a long time the geyser does not differ from an ordinary hot spring. But finally, the tube grows so long that the water at the surface is comparatively cold, while that at the bottom is boiling. The column of water in the tube is increased by the flow from adjoining hot springs which drain into it, and under its weight a large volume of steam, under great pressure, is generated in the lower part of the tube. This pressure finally becomes sufficiently great to force up a quantity of the water so that it overflows from the tube. The removal of the weight of this water, results in a large body of the confined water bursting into steam, which rushes to the surface through the tube, carrying with it the column of water, which it hurls into air on reaching the surface.

This is the best authority, and therefore must not be disputed. Still, it will be observed that very frequently the quantity of water which is actually thrown out of the tube before the eruption commences is little or nothing. Probably, however, enough is thrown out to permit steam to be formed before it can flow back. There is quite a difference between the temperature of the different springs and geysers, and even of the water from the same geyser at different periods. Their altitude is so much greater than the sea level, that the boiling point is ten to fifteen degrees below 212° Fahr. The water of "Old Faithful" and the "Bee Hive," is 200° Fahr.; that of the "Grand" is 189° Fahr.; the "Turban" 195° Fahr.; and "Castle" and "Giant," 193° to 194° Fahr. The taste of the water we did not find to be disagreeable when it was cold, and it was not unwholesome.

The much talked of geysers of Iceland are of little importance compared with those of the Yellowstone, their highest eruption being from about sixty to seventy feet, while those of the Yellowstone frequently exceed two hundred feet in height.

CHAPTER XVI.

THE RIDE TO THE CAÑON.

I had originally intended, after visiting the main points of interest in the Park, to go into a wild section on the north-eastern side, known as the Hoodoo country, to hunt for elk and bear. We had learned, however, that the miners from the adjoining mining camps had killed off all the game in that section, and I had therefore decided to return to Bozeman *via* the Madison Basin, which is to the north-west of the Park, and try my fortunes by a hunt in the mountains surrounding it, although this would prolong our trip more than we had anticipated.

For several days Fisher had been anxiously watching for an acquaintance named Jack Cole, who had a cabin in the Madison Basin, and from whom he had expected to obtain the latest information in regard to game. This Jack Cole was a typical plainsman. An old buffalo hunter when the buffalo existed, he had been a scout for Generals Howard and Miles in their Indian campaigns. Having killed four men in various little difficulties, he enjoyed a reputation among frontiersmen such as Sullivan has in Boston. At present, he was engaged in the prosaic occupation of supplying fish and game to the hotels in the Park.

While Fisher and I were riding ahead of our party, on the day after leaving the great Geysers, and were discussing the chances of meeting the redoubtable Cole, we saw a wagon approaching, driven by a big, fresh complexioned man, with a broad brimmed hat. Presently, Fisher exclaimed, "Why, there he is," and galloped off, I following him. As we neared the wagon, Fisher, who was always quick in his motions, reined in his horse, jumped off and ran hastily up to the wagon. Its occupant produced a big revolver like a flash, but the next instant, recognizing Fisher, restored it to its hiding place in the wagon, and in reply to the questions put him, gave us full information of where to camp and where to hunt.

After his departure, I asked Fisher what made Cole reach for his pistol so promptly.

"Well, you see," said Fisher, "a man like that never knows at what time some friend of some of the fellows he has shot may go for him and he wants to get the first shot. Then, besides, he may have had some little difficulty with the law and don't care to be arrested. I guess he thought I was a sheriff. It was funny to see him reach for his pistol, wasn't it?"

"Yes," I replied, "funny for me but scarcely so funny for you."

Our route was towards the forks of the Firehole by the same road we had come over. Just before reaching the river we turned off to the east upon the road to the Grand Cañon. This wound along the banks of the east branch of the Firehole, which here runs through a narrow valley with steep walls. Some ten miles from the Forks we emerged into a grassy prairie, and saw in front of us the steep face of the high "divide," or plateau, through which the cañon of the Yellowstone has been cut. The road up this is a graded road and well laid out. It zig-zags up the mountain side so as to make the ascent as easy as possible, and although somewhat rough, is probably in as good a condition as such a road could be expected to be. But nevertheless, to ascend it was a tremendous climb, and one which was hard on the horses. The view from it, however, was magnificent, overlooking the entire valley below and showing the vast snow-clad peaks of the Rocky Mountains which closed the horizon as far as the eye could reach.

A short distance beyond the summit we passed a pretty little sheet of water known as "Mary's Lake," where we lunched, having then ridden about twenty miles, much of it hard climbing. The lake water was brackish and tepid, but with cold coffee, beer, and a canteen of cool water, which our military friends always carried in the wagon, we were independent of it.

A short distance further we passed Sulphur Lake—a small lake with several hot springs around it, all so impregnated with sulphur as to make quite a disagreeable odor.

Just beyond this we crossed Alum Creek, a little stream into which so many chemical springs flow as to make it utterly unfit for use by man or animal. In places it was so full of alum as to be green. We relied upon what we were told and its looks as to its qualities, and did not taste it.

After reaching the summit of the Divide, the country changes to a table land, somewhat rolling, but usually level. For a long way the road passes through a series of "parks," as they are termed—small prairies extending a quarter of a mile on either hand, bordered by handsome woods and covered with a luxuriant growth of grass. It seemed difficult to believe as we rode along that we were not traversing a gentleman's country seat, and that at the next turn in the road some elegant building would not come in sight.

These parks are a favorite resort for bear in search of ant hills and roots. I kept a close watch in the hopes of seeing some, but was disappointed. There is so much travel over all the main roads of the Park that the game keeps aloof from them, and my rifle might as well have been in the wagon. If it had been, however, I would probably have seen any quantity of game, as that is a

sportsman's usual luck.   The forests here are much more
attractive than those in the valleys below.   The trees are
larger and afford more shade, and the absence of underbrush enables the eye to penetrate the recesses for a long
distance, thus adding to the park-like appearance to the
scene.

Finally, we reached Sage or Little Trout Creek, which,
although a spring, and not a creek, was cool and fresh.
As we had then ridden twenty-seven miles we were all
tired enough to stop, so we halted and pitched our camp
on the slope of a little hill adjoining the creek.

Here we met mosquitoes for the first time, but to us
they were not particularly annoying.

I had heard terrible things about the insects to be encountered in the Park during July ; and had gone fully
equipped with mosquito curtains, head nets, and last, but
not least, "fly medicine," made according to my own
receipt of tar oil, sweet oil, with a little castor oil and a
few drops of carbolic acid added, which experience had
convinced me would keep off anything in the shape of
insects.   But to the sportsman who is familiar with the
mosquitoes of the Adirondacks, of New Jersey, or with
those of the south side of Long Island, those of the
Park are beneath contempt.   Although I always carried
a vial of fly medicine, I did not use it three times during
the trip.   We never used our head nets, and only put up the
mosquito curtains in our tent half a dozen times.   Our
men complained more than we did, probably because they
did not know how bad Eastern mosquitoes are.   I met
some friends, however, who complained that they were
annoyed a great deal by mosquitoes around the Cañon
about sun down, so that they were forced to build a
"smudge" for protection.   At night it was too cold for
mosquitoes to be about.

The horse-flies were very numerous along this plateau ;
and although they did not bite us they annoyed the horses

greatly. When we picketed the latter in the afternoon we smeared them plentifully with our fly medicine, and found it of great value, as it enabled them to graze in peace.

Early on the 25th of July we left camp for the Cañon. After a ride of about five miles we passed a sign-board showing where the trail to the Yellowstone Lake turned off from the road we were following. We looked in that direction with longing eyes, but it was impossible to spare the time to visit the lake unless I gave up the idea of going on a projected hunting excursion, which I was unwilling to do. It was quite a sacrifice to turn away without visiting this lake, as the scenery around it is very fine, with innumerable paint pots and curious springs, making it well worth a visit, and I was told by the army officers that the fishing was magnificent.

It is along this lake that an angler can catch a trout, and, without changing his position or removing the fish from the hook, cook him by dropping him into a boiling spring. The same thing can also be done on the Gardner River. This seems absurd ; but I know gentlemen who have done it.

After leaving Sage Creek, the road passes over bare prairies and is uninteresting until the Sulphur Mountains are reached. These consist of several cone-shaped hills about one hundred and fifty feet high and composed almost entirely of sulphur. Their surface is broken with numerous small vent holes from which little jets of sulphurous steam are constantly rising, which, as it condenses, covers the ground surrounding them with bright yellow crystals. We broke off some pieces, and found them too hot to hold in the hand.

Around the base of these mountains are grouped a number of hot springs which also emit sulphurous fumes. Some of these are very large. One which is about fifteen by twenty feet square, boils most furiously, throwing up the water four or five feet high, and at the same time having a curious tide-like raising and falling, now filling its whole basin to the edge and then receding several feet. Great clouds of vapor roll out from this boiling water, so strongly impregnated with sulphur as to make it impossible to approach near to it. A short distance further is an immense caldron over fifty feet in diameter, whose dirty slate-colored water constantly boils with a fury which keeps it leaping into wave-like jets. A short distance from this is a space of several acres where there are some thirty mud springs clustered together, usually of a dull brown color, although some are white and others pink. They are about the consistency of mush and boil slowly ; from time to time some subterranean force, either gas or steam, is seen bursting through them in great bubbles, sometimes with a force which throws their contents several feet into the air. One spring of black mud was under such a pressure as caused it to eject its mud a long distance. The Blue Mud Pot is twenty feet in diameter, and full of mud so fine that when the puffs of steam or gas rise through it (which they do with an odor of sulphurated hydrogen) the surface undulates in regular pulsations, or rings, as when a stone is thrown into a pond. All around these springs and pots the ground is perfectly barren. The bare and baked earth, the caldrons of boiling, bubbling mud, of variegated hue, and the sulphurous clouds of steam, made a most "uncanny" looking place ; one of those curiosities which one is glad to see, but leaves with a feeling of relief.

CHAPTER XVII.

THE GREAT CAÑON OF THE YELLOWSTONE.

A few miles beyond this delectable spot we reached the Yellowstone and drew rein to let our horses drink from its cool and pure waters. Unlike the rapid torrent we had previously seen, it was here a broad, and very clear stream, with a swift but still current, unbroken by rock or rapid. On the opposite side the banks were hilly, but on the left bank where we were, they were low and grassy. The river was so clear that it seemed as if it could be forded, and we were told that several lives had been lost in attempting to do so.

The road runs along the left bank of the stream until near the Falls, which were about two miles below. From where we were, onward down the river, the scenery becomes more rugged. The mountains begin to close in upon the swiftly moving river until they contract its width over one-half, producing so great pressure as to force the water into great rapids and cascades, resembling those above Goat Island at Niagara, in which turbulent shape it tears along through rocky gorges and over huge ledges with resistless power, until it takes its tremendous leap into the Cañon below.

We found a pleasant little glade at the edge of the river, just below the commencement of the rapids, which we selected for a camping ground. A portion of the party rode on to view the Great Cañon, while I occupied myself with the more prosaic duty of seeing that the camp was put in order, and catching some fish for supper. Climbing down into a little recess or bay formed by two huge projecting rocks, and fronting on an eddy where the rapids rounded into their first cascade, I found splendid sport. The trout, some of which weighed over two pounds, rose freely at dark flies, and a yellowish brown coachman (a very taking fly for all Montana). Here, for the first time, I found " wormy " trout.

It seems that the trout found in the Yellowstone Lake, and in that portion of the river extending to the Upper Falls, are afflicted with a parasite or species of grub, said by Professor Leidy to be *Dibothrium Cordiceps* (which is very gratifying to know). These were usually found under the pectoral fin (what in a man would be the arm pit), and seemed to eat away its substance, as a bug would eat a vine leaf. The smaller trout appeared to be unaffected, but one half of those weighing in the neighborhood of a pound had more or less of these worms, while the fins of almost all trout of a larger size were quite badly eaten by them. The presence of these parasites seems to affect both the health and strength of the larger fish. A gamy trout which fought hard and looked plump and bright colored, when taken out of the water, would have few, if any, worms upon him. But when a big fish would rise with a great splash, and after making one or two fierce rushes when hooked, suddenly cease to resist and allow himself to be drawn in with no opposition beyond a sullen "flop" of his tail, like a pickerel, he would be found to be sallow, slab-sided, and to have his pectoral fins almost eaten off. We were unable to find that these worms penetrated the body of the fish (although scientific men say they do), and therefore the men of the party did not hesitate to eat such trout as appeared fat and healthy looking, whether worms were found upon their fins or not, being only careful to see that they were thoroughly cooked, as we learned from the soldiers that on their previous visits all their party had eaten them without injury. No difference could be discerned between the taste of these and of any other trout, and finally even the ladies were induced to eat them. What causes the presence of these worms, neither learned professors nor practical guides have the slightest idea.

Very curiously, these worms are found only upon the fish in the Yellowstone Lake and in that part of the Yellowstone River which extends from the Lake to the Falls. In all the rest of the river the trout are uncommonly vigorous and healthy looking, and are without a sign of a worm ever having been upon any of them. At Tower Falls, which is only a few miles below the Great Falls, fish are caught of six or seven pounds weight and which are as healthy and game as it is possible for trout to be.

Why it is that these parasites, or fish infested with them, should not be carried over the Falls and down the river, so that the other fish would be affected, is something that I am unable to explain.

Having caught enough fish for several meals in a short time, I gave up the sport and rode after the rest of the party, who had gone on to the Great Cañon. The wagon road stopped about a mile from our camp, where the stage station or hotel is situated. This is a kind of permanent camp, composed of large tents, or more properly, small canvas houses with blankets for portieres, and an extra large tent for a dining-room. It appeared to be well kept and comfortable for such a structure.

Beyond the hotel the path is a narrow trail through the woods and skirting the river, just wide enough for a horse to pass over. It is safe enough, but those who are not accustomed to the saddle will find their minds much more at ease if they traverse it on foot instead of on horseback, as it winds down and up slopes of forty-five degrees, over pole bridges and along rude embankments overhanging steep cañons in rather a surprising manner.

On the way, Cascade Creek is crossed. The bridge over it is a substantial log structure, but the trail leads to and from it at an abrupt descent and turns at the bottom in a very sharp angle. There is a beautiful pool here known as "Grotto Pool," and a picturesque little fall, but these are completely eclipsed by the wonders of the Cañon beyond.

Riding up the steep path from the Creek and through a fringe of trees, the visitor suddenly finds himself within a yard of the edge of a precipice a thousand feet deep, and without the slightest protection to keep him from falling over it.

Two weeks in the saddle had toughened our nerves and inspired us with the fullest confidence in our steeds, but riding over parts of this trail severely tested both. The ladies sustained the strain with heroism, only occasionally on our return, as we approached some peculiarly formidable descent, I could hear a faint "Oh, *Gracious!*" behind me, which expressed volumes. Yet, on a second trip; they did not appear to mind these experiences in the least.

Continuing along the trail and close to the dizzy depths of the cañon, I finally reached my party, who were gathered on a projecting cliff known as Point Lookout, and which is two miles below the hotel.

Here, for the first time, I enjoyed a good view of one of the grandest sights in the world, the Great Cañon of the Yellowstone. No one who has ever seen this majestic creation of nature can forget it, but to adequately describe the scene is beyond the power of language.

For a mile or so from the place where we had camped, the cliffs increased in height and hem in the river more closely, forcing the water into more and more turbulent rapids and cascades, until at the Upper Fall the water is confined into a chasm of eighty feet in width, with banks from two to three hundred feet high. The torrent rushes over this Fall with an impetuous sweep, and drops with a sheer descent of one hundred and twelve feet in an un-

LOWER FALLS OF THE YELLOWSTONE.

broken sheet upon a huge rock below, with a shock which throws up great clouds of spray, nearly to the summit of the Fall above the water, forming an immense whirl-pool, which slowly circles at the foot of the Fall. Emerging from this, the river tears like a mad thing, breaking into rapids and cascades, for half a mile further, between rocky cliffs, which grow constantly higher and higher, until it hurls itself over the Great Fall, in an appalling leap of three hundred feet, and then plunges in a succession of cascade after cascade, into the dark abyss of the Great Cañon.

The point where we stood afforded a magnificent view of both the Great Fall and the Cañon, although it required some nerve to enjoy the prospect, and most of the party showed a decided inclination to keep a firm grip upon something solid while looking at it.

On the right was the Great or Lower Fall, the water dark blue on the surface of the river above, and changing into a huge snow-white curve as it made its vast plunge of three hundred feet (higher than the piers of the Brooklyn Bridge and double the height of Niagara), and terminating in an enormous fountain of spray, from which huge clouds of mist rolled far up the cañon, and through which a beautiful rainbow could at times be seen.

But the Cañon itself was so stupendous that the Fall, grand as it was, formed but an incident to it.

Far beneath, and to each side of us, extended a vast gorge or cleft in the mountains more than a thousand feet deep, a thousand yards wide at the top, and narrowing at the bottom to almost nothing; so deep that the river below seemed like a green ribbon, flecked here and there with patches of white; and great trees below appeared no larger than one's finger. The sides were perpendicular cliffs, like five rows of the Palisades of the Hudson, set one above another. These were not simply naked stone, such as is seen in other cañons, but were of the most variegated and startling hues, partly caused by the natural colors of the rocks, partly from the different mosses and algæ, which are nourished by the mists of the falls, and partly from the action of hot springs, which had formed different colored deposits through the ages that had been occupied by the water in wearing out this huge passage through the rocks. On one side would be a vast cliff of a pale pink ; adjoining it, another of buff, and opposite, a promontory of purple. Red, yellow, orange and brown were all visible at once, and beneath all ran the river, changing from blue to green, and flecked with white cascades. On the right side, just below the falls, was a great bank of snow, the size of a house. The sun was shining brightly, but the snow lay far below where its rays could penetrate. At each change in the sunlight these colors would change almost like a kaleidoscope, making it almost impossible to sketch them.

Here and there along the sides of the Cañon projected huge rocks, forming pinnacles of great hight, which had been moulded by the elements into grotesque shapes, some resembling steeples, and one like a minaret. Yet, tall as they are, they were dwarfed by the vast abyss in which they ware situated.

The Cañon extends for some twenty-four miles, winding and turning so that but a short portion of it could be seen from any point. At each turn the scene changed. At one place the walls of the Cañon were perpendicular, at another they extended with an even slope from the brink above to the edge of the river, and at a third they were broken into projecting crags and peaks, which rose one above the other to the level of the plateau above.

At all times several eagles were slowly circling through this dizzy gorge, but looking like sparrows in the immensity around them. One of them had built its nest on a knob which surmounted a pinnacle just below us.

The silence, the depth, and the vastness of the scene were overpowering.

We sat and gazed in silence, for words could not do justice to our feelings. The impressiveness of the scene may be judged from its effect upon one of our soldiers, as narrated by himself. "When I first saw the Cañon," said he, "I just sat still for a straight hour and looked at it without saying a word;" and then after a pause he added with great emphasis, *"and it was dinner time, too."*

Few not familiar with army life will appreciate the full force of this tribute to the wonders of the scene.

I should have greatly liked to have climbed down into the Cañon, but there is no way to do so. It is to be hoped that it will not be long before some method will be devised by which visitors can descend into its depths, for the view from below must be even more impressive than from above. Much of the stone and débris which forms the slopes of the sides of the Cañon, where there are any slopes, is so loose that it would be impossible to climb them. A stone which a man can throw with one hand will, on striking, dislodge quite a quantity of it.

It is possible to climb down the bed of Cascade Creek to the river, between the Upper and Lower Falls, and good fishing is to be had there. A steep path also extends from the trail along the edge of the cliff, to a platform which has been built close to the edge of the Great Fall, but no better view is to be had from this than from the cliff above, as the clouds of mist from the falling water hide the view of the fall. The rush and sweep of the water as viewed from this platform are, however, very fine.

While we were still enjoying the view, dark clouds came up and it began to sprinkle, so as to render it prudent to return to camp. It was well we did so, for soon a light rain was falling, the first and only one we encountered in the Park.

During the night the weather cleared and there was a

heavy frost, ice forming in our pails and my landing net freezing stiff. I was told of one guest at the hotel who slept under sixteen blankets ! He would have done much better if he had used a quarter of the number and spread a rubber coat on top, which would have kept in the heat. At this great altitude, 7,800 feet above the sea (which far exceeds that of Mount Washington), cold nights are quite common, and snow may be expected during September or even the end of August. But the clearness and the purity of the air are indescribable. Throughout the trip it was most exhilarating to expand the lungs to their fullest extent and drink in the air, and we found ourselves constantly doing it to enjoy the sensation. In fact, for some time after our return home the air seemed heavy and oppressive.

We all rode up to the Cañon in the morning, as the shower would tend to bring out more vividly its colors. There had not been sufficient rain to effect much alteration, but the change in the position of the sun had altered the light so as to give quite different effects from those we had seen the previous evening. My daughter endeavored to produce a water color sketch that would afford some idea, at least, of the colors ; but she found that every stone and rock required to be painted separately, while the hues were altering with each change of light, and after working faithfully all the forenoon she gave up in despair, and said it would require a month to reproduce the scene, even roughly.

She consoled herself, however, for this disappointment by executing a little waltz upon the little rocky platform from which she had been sketching, and which projected over the depths of the Cañon, to the speechless horror of her mother.

After dinner I set out up the river for some trout. The eddy where I fished on the day of our arrival had been since fished so steadily with flies and bait by the members of our own party and those of another which had camped near us, that it had been cleaned out. For some distance above it the banks were rocky and so steep and high that fly-fishing was an impossibility, although large trout could be seen lying in the water at their base. Beyond them the left bank of the river was low, grassy and free from trees or bushes, just the place to throw a fly. I strolled along it for nearly half a mile, throwing out into the stream, which here is clear and smooth, although with quite a current, and dropping my flies into the eddies below several logs and rocks where trout were likely to be. Not a single rise, however, rewarded my exertions. Finally, I reached a place where the river set back into a sort of bayou. This was only some two feet deep, without eddy or current, and was so clear that the bottom was distinctly visible for a distance of from fifty to sixty feet from the shore. It was the last place trout would naturally be expected to be found, or to rise to a lure if they were there. More for the pleasure which an enthusiastic angler experiences in making a long cast than with any idea of actually obtaining a rise, I lengthened my line and threw out some sixty feet. The instant the flies touched the water, there was a great swirl and splash which was met with a quick turn of the wrist, and the fish was hooked. My rod bent double, and the reel fairly buzzed as he ran straight away, and then from side to side, occasionally leaping clear out of the water in his frantic efforts to break loose. After an exciting struggle, the steady pressure of the " split bambo " rod, finally overpowered him, and he was drawn sullenly to the shore, resisting to the last, until Horace deftly inserted the landing net under him. He weighed nearly two pounds, and a gamer fish I have never caught.

Inspired by this success, I threw again around the point, and caught another fish weighing a pound. About this time I heard feminine shrieks mingled with laughter be-

VIEWS IN THE GREAT CAÑON.

hind me. Turning, I saw my wife and daughter were following me down the bank, fishing over the same ground where I had such ill success, and were each playing a large trout whose struggles threatened to bring their lines into contact, and rendered them wild with excitement.

I turned towards them and for an hour we stood on the bank within a hundred feet of each other and caught trout averaging about a pound in weight, almost as fast as we could land them, all of whom, unlike those caught previously were as gamy as Adirondack trout. There seemed to be a school of fish about thirty feet out in the river. The ladies, however, had become sufficiently expert to be able to throw a fly that distance, and whenever they did so, they were sure to get a rise. They lost a number of fish, either from not "striking" with sufficient rapidity, or from being too much in a hurry to land them, after they were hooked—the error into which unexperienced fishermen are so apt to fall, and from which, in my judgment, more fish are lost than from any other reason. Still, they made a great catch, and fished until they became too tired to longer throw a fly.

Altogether, in an hour and a half we had landed twenty-eight trout that weighed over a pound each, and could have caught more. The most killing fly appeared to be a black fly for a tail fly, and either a yellow with white wings or a gray fly for a dropper. The two former resemble flies which were flying around the river banks. Yet, although there were plenty of white millers also to be seen, the trout would not look at an artificial one ; neither would they rise to a red ibis, which I had found to be a killing fly down the river.

That night was one of the loveliest of our trip. The moon was full, and its bright light was reflected from the dancing water of the rapids and cascades in front of our camp, making them look like burnished silver. It shone softly through the trees, lighting up each little glade, deepening the shadows of the forest and bringing out our white tents into vivid contrast. A large camp fire added its ruddy light to the romantic scene, and we sat around it until quite late, enjoying the beauty of the scene, listening to the ladies exalt their fishing exploits and to the ceaseless sounds of the rushing river.

It became very cold during the night, causing quite a fog from the river, as it is so common in mountain regions, so that in the morning everything was covered with a white frost, making walking through the long grass after the stock far from agreeable. But as soon as the sun got up over the mountains it became warm and comfortable.

We came quite near having a severe accident on this morning. The horses had become well rested by the two day's rest and the good grazing they had enjoyed, and were quite fresh. While Fisher was leading two of them to the camp by their picket ropes, one became frightened at something or other he saw, or imagined he saw, and bolted in such a manner as to get a turn of the rope around Fisher's neck, and it was only by the exertion of great coolness and strength that the latter was able to prevent himself from being strangled. As it was, his right hand was quite badly cut by the rope.

If we had not been pressed for time, we should have continued on to the top of Mount Washburn. This is about twelve miles from the Falls and is reached by a good trail, so that one can ride to the summit. This is 10,000 feet above the sea, and from it a magnificent view of the whole Park can be obtained.

Some of a party that I met rode up there, and said that it more than repaid them for the trip. Those who go that way keep on and return to the Mammoth Springs by way of Tower Falls, a distance of about twenty one miles. Those who do not do so return by way of the Forks of the Firehole River.

IN THE THIRD CAÑON.

Although we did not wish to pass over the same ground twice, yet we were compelled to adopt that course, as we did not intend to return to the Mammoth Springs.

Fisher's mishap delayed us somewhat, so that it was eight o'clock before we were on the road back to the Forks of the Firehole. The day was cool and bracing; we and our horses were both refreshed by the two days rest, and we had a magnificent ride. When, after fording the river, we reached the open prairies, the fresh breeze that swept over them inspirited the ponies so that they were wild to go; and for several miles we had some quite exciting races. I can assure those who have only spent their vacations at fashionable watering places, or in dull country villages, that they would experience a new sensation if they should mount a spirited horse and gallop at full speed over a rolling prairie, in the high altitudes of the Rocky Mountains, where the pure air and rapid motion stirs the blood like a trumpet. Even now, as I recall such incidents, the old fervor comes back, and it seems as if my fingers held the reins instead of a pen; and I once more felt the exhilarating breeze of the prairie in my face, and with bounding pulse swayed again in the saddle to the gallop of my horse.

Although we stopped two hours on the road for lunch, we made such progress that we were at our old camp on the Firehole at four o'clock, the distance being thirty miles; and this was accomplished without fatigue. Here we met a tremendous "out-fit" of tourists, forty strong, with an array of stages, baggage-wagons, tents, horses and attendants, resembling a traveling circus. But there appeared to be no head, and no management. Some wanted to go one way and some another; consequently they were quarreling among themselves; their men were dissatisfied because they could not give satisfaction, and everything appeared to be going wrong.

A large party is always a difficult thing to manage,

particularly in camp. But there is only one way to do it, and that is to have some one person appointed from the outset as the sole leader, who shall be vested with absolute authority, and who shall alone give orders to the employees.

While at this camp, we heard with great regret that the gallant fight against death which General Grant had fought so long and so stubbornly was ended, and that he had gone to his rest. While all were glad that his sufferings were ended, the news was received with sadness, and cast quite a gloom over our party in particular, several of whom, including myself, had the honor of his personal acquaintance. The intelligence came by telegraph to the Mammoth Springs, and was forwarded from there by the stages; so that we knew it at the Firehole on July 27, only four days after it took place.

CHAPTER XVIII.

THE FORMER INHABITANTS OF THE PARK.

The visitor to the Park is naturally desirous of learning something in regard to the habits and fate of its original inhabitants, and it would be scarcely fitting that a description of the Park should be closed without some reference being made to them. The story, however, is a brief one.

In early years the territory surrounding the Park was the hunting grounds of various tribes of Indians, including the Crows, Shoshones and Bannocks. Their hostility long kept white men in ignorance of its wonders, but it is probable that their superstitious awe of the spouting geysers prevented them from frequently visiting it themselves. Its real occupants were a small tribe of Indians known as "Sheep-eaters," from their use of the flesh and skin of the big-horned sheep for food and clothing. The "Sheep-eaters" were in a very low state of civilization. They had few, if any, horses, no firearms, and until within a few years, had no iron weapons. Their knives and axes were made of Obsidan or volcanic glass, so that the poles and stumps of trees which they have cut appear as if gnawed by beavers. They constructed no permanent habitations, but dwelt in caves, or nearly inaccessible niches in the cliffs, occasionally, however, making little circular upright bush heaps called "wickeups," a number of which are yet seen around the Mammoth Hot Springs, in the basins, and along the Yellowstone Lake. They were in the habit of building extensive pole or brush fences as driveways for deer, bison, and other animals, leading to places in the various passes which were within the reach of their rude lances and Obsidan headed arrows. These driveways were mainly constructed of fallen saplings, which being pitchy, have remained without decaying, so that even at the present time they can be traced for a long distance. One of these driveways is now plainly visible upon the southern cliff of the cañon of the West Gardner. Beyond these few structures, these Indians have left fewer enduring evidences of their occupancy than the beaver, badger, and other animals upon which they subsisted.

The NesPercés made a raid in the Park in 1877, and killed and wounded a number of tourists, among whom was Professor Dietrich. On this raid they also killed a number of miners from the Black Hills region, whose skeletons were found on the line of retreat of the fleeing band. In 1879, there were no Indian raids, but the Sheep-eaters, with a few raiding bands of Bannocks and Shoshones, made the possession of animals in the Park rather uncertain, although they killed no white men. Since that time the Indian difficulty has been cured, the Indians have been forced back on their distant reservations, and the traveller in the Park will see or hear no more of them than if he was in the Adirondacks or White Mountains.

CHAPTER XIX.

THE MADISON BASIN.

The following day we parted with great regret from our agreeable army friends, whose leave had expired and who were compelled to return by Yankee Jim's road, through which we had originally entered the Park. Our own route lay in a different direction. The road we took is that which is used by those who enter the Park from the Central Pacific Railroad, and although not a *very* bad road for the woods, was the worst we had so far encountered in our trip. Passing in rear of the hotel, it ascended a steep mountain composed of a loose, sandy sort of formation, very much like the mountains around the Mammoth Springs, making it hard pulling for a loaded wagon. Then came a succession of quite pretty glades and woods, and then an almost interminable stretch through a burnt forest of bull pine ; a straight avenue extending as far as the eye could reach, and apparently lined on each side with telegraph poles standing as thick as they could be placed, but all scarred and blackened. With the exception of a space cleared for the wheel tracks, the stumps stood thickly in some parts of the road, and the cheerless prospect was not helped by the hot sun and the absence of shade.

It was not agreeable to a horseman, and I was told that those who passed over it in the stages from the Central Pacific Railroad, found this portion of it to be atrocious.

After riding some two hours through this depressing scene we emerged upon the edge of the Madison Basin, where a most magnificent view burst upon us. We stood upon the brink of a steep mountain. Two thousand feet below us spread a wide level valley covered with timber, through which in various places the blue waters of the Madison River could be seen glimmering in the sunshine. Far in front of us, and on either hand was a circle of high mountains, the true Rockies, covered with purple forests up to "timber line," while far above them towered bare and rocky peaks, rosy in the sunlight and streaked here and there with huge patches of snow.

The road from the summit where we were zigzagged down the mountain, sometimes at quite a sharp grade and frequently overhanging the verge of a precipitous cañon from which we could look over the tree tops of the valley below. As it was quite narrow, the horsemen rode well ahead to give warning of any appraching teams as well as to look out for game, for we were now in a section where the latter might be encountered.

Suddenly, as we turned a sharp curve we came upon a wagon without horses, standing in a narrow place in the road, by the side of which stood a woman holding a baby, two little children and a dog—no one else.

I had been keeping a bright lookout all the morning for game, and should not have been surprised to have been suddenly met by a bear or an elk. But to encounter a woman and children in such a place was certainly unexpected. The first question was how are we going to get past their outfit. Fisher rode hastily back to stop the wagon, and bring down Sam, to see what conld be done, although it did not seem to me as if there was any possibility of our wagon passing. When Sam arrived and examined the situation with the eye of a professional, he decided at once that while there was no room to spare he could get through, and he did, one wheel just grazing the hubs of the other wagon, and the other going within two inches of the edge of the cañon, the road crumbling under the outside wheel in one place in a way which was far from agreeable.

While this all was going on, the ladies of our party were conversing with the proprietress of the obstructing outfit. She was dressed in calico, with a sunbonnet. Her two little girls, who were from three to five years of age, were dressed in short skirts of gingham, with little trousers of similar material. Their shoes were good, and all the party were clean and neat, as well as everything about the wagon. The woman said her husband had taken the horses down the cañon to water them, and they were awaiting his return ; that they had come from Walla Walla in Washington Territory, (about 900 miles) and were going to the States (1,000 to 1,200 miles more) and they thought they would "take in" the Park on the trip (which involved an additional drive of at least 400 miles.)

"It was a little out of their way," she said, "but they thought they might better take it in as they passed this time (?) they might not come this way again, and would never see it if they didn't."

In the course of the conversation it came out that she had been traveling for fifteen summers looking for a home to *suit* her, that none of her children had been born in a house, that she had educated them herself, and the eldest was in the Fifth Reader. Notwithstanding her experiences, her language and manners were refined and cultivated, in fact, she was a lady. If I had met her in the East I should have taken her to be a school teacher. We were told at places where her party had camped, that they had reduced it to a system, and that small as were the children, each had their allotted task with which they were perfectly familiar. One bringing wood, while the other made the fire, etc.

They were certainly one of the most independent families I ever encountered.

We found that there was through the West a class of what may be termed "professional emigrants."

Possessed with a desire to roam, they never seem to establish themselves permanently in any place, but wander from the East to the West, and then back "to the States," as the humor strikes them. It must not, however, be understood that they are tramps or anything like it. On the contrary, they are self-supporting and marvelously independent.

About noon we reached an abandoned log stable on the banks of the Madison, known as Fourteen Mile Station, which had once been used as a stage stable.

As I rode around the rear of the building I found a buckboard wagon standing in front of the doorway, across the seat of which lay a Winchester rifle. Seated on the doorsill was Mr. Jack Cole, peacefully reading a pamphlet "History of England." I noticed, however, that his Winchester was placed so that its butt was within easy reach of his hand, and that a heavy revolver protruded from the hip pocket of his canvas overalls. He was large and stout, with blonde complexion, a heavy yellow mustache, and a long goatee, and looked like a German brewer, except that his hair was as long as a woman's, and was twisted up into a knot at the back of his head. He wore a heavy broad brimmed hat with a band composed of heavy figured silk cord, braided in a taper like a whip lash so that it was an inch thick in front, and narrow behind. His other attire was not peculiar. His voice was low and quiet, and he was very polite, particularly to the ladies. We chatted with him for some time while we were eating our lunch and enjoying our noontide rest. He mourned sadly over the disappearance of game from the country.

"It is no use any longer," he said sorrowfully, "for a man to carry a rifle in Montana, and I suppose old hunters like me will soon have to starve." Still, he denounced

---

JACK COLE.

the recently enacted game laws of the Territory. "They were only passed in the interest of a set of foreign dudes —British aristocrats who cared for nothing but themselves," and he narrated with evident enjoyment, how he and some other old buffalo hunters, who had been warned by the agents of some of those gentlemen to desist from hunting, had served notice upon the gentlemen themselves to leave the country, which notice the latter had been wise enough to obey.

He was now engaged in carrying fish from Henry's Lake to the hotel at the "Upper Geyser Basin," and had on his wagon a box as large as a trunk, which was full of great trout, some of which he insisted upon our taking. He drank a glass of beer with us, but evidently only as a matter of politeness and refused anything else. He greatly dampened our hopes of fishing by assuring us that the trout in the lake would not rise to a fly (in which he was in error), and he pointed out the places where I would be likely to find elk. He also told us where to find a spring down the river to camp by, and showed us how to open a beer bottle by tapping the neck with the back of a knife, the neck breaking after a few upward taps. Sam at once opened a bottle in that way, and having poured out the beer, replaced it with water, restored the cork and neck, and put the bottle where a traveller would, as he said, "be likely to be made happy by thinking he had found a bottle of beer."

No one seeing Cole sitting there, perfectly self-possessed, talking in his quiet way, would have imagined that he was anything of a desperado.

I was afterwards told that many of the frontiersmen who have killed a number of men are "more sinned against than sinning." It was explained in this way:

"A fight out here, in past days particularly, means a fight with pistols. A man gets in a brawl, pistols are drawn and he kills some one. If this is done fairly, no

one thinks much of it. Then suppose this man is unlucky enough to get into another difficulty and again
kills a man. From that time he commences to be known
and talked about, and becomes in constant danger of an
attack from the friends of the man he has shot, and still
more from a certain class of ' rustlers ' who are desirous
of earning a reputation as a ' man-killer ' for themselves
by shooting somebody who bears the reputation of being
one, just as Eastern pugilists are constantly trying to
knock out John L. Sullivan. The knowledge of this
keeps the man always on the alert, he seldom drinks to
excess, is always prepared to defend himself, and he constantly studies how to shoot accurately and above all,
quickly. Consequently, any one who does tackle him is
pretty certain to get the worst of it. In this way, a man
without desiring it in the least, may be actually forced
into killing a number of others."

For example, Fisher told me that he had seen a man
in a saloon shoot at Cole, who had merely warned the
shooter that if he fired again he would kill him, and
actually waited until the man had fired a second time
before he returned the fire, when he shot his assailant
dead.

In the course of the conversation the remark was made
that the men that were managing the new hotel at the
"Upper Geysers" had suspended payment, the season
having been late and visitors few. It seemed that they
were in arrears to Cole, and he at once showed that he
did not propose to lose his money.

He led out his bronchos and "hitched up" with great
promptness, being very careful, we observed, to handle
gingerly a gray, who he declared had a habit of shaking
hands with his hind leg, and left us with the assurance
"that he was either going to collect that bill, or to run
that hotel until he got his money back."

As he departed over the hill, the little knob into which

his long back hair was twisted, showed to its best advantage under his sombrero, and was, as the ladies declared, "just too funny for anything."

He was to return by way of our camp in a day or two, but did not, and our burning curiosity as to what he did at the hotel was never satisfied. We were glad, however, that it was some one other than us that owed him the money.

The camping place Cole had pointed out was on the bottom, below the ridge along which the road ran, and was only seven miles from where we had met him, so that we reached it early in the afternoon. We pitched our camp under some trees not far from a cool spring, which comes out of the bank close to the river. While the men were putting out the horses, a large crane flew along the river and lit in the water about 150 yards from us, which I killed with my rifle, making quite a neat shot.

We were just getting settled when two men rode down the bank from the road, and made some inquiries in regard to the road which were absurd on their face. Their questions were evidently a mere cover for something else, and their appearance was suspicious. They were well mounted, but without equipment for camping. One rode a valuable young horse with a brand-new bridle, but without a saddle !

"Horse thieves," Jim remarked to me in an undertone. "We must look out for the stock to-night."

Our party, however, was too strong and experienced, and there were too many weapons standing around within reach to have made it safe for two men to trouble us in the daytime. Still, we were careful to always keep that number of men around the camp so long as we stayed there. In the afternoon we fished the river. It appeared promising, although a little warm, but the trout were small and scarce.

In going through the brush we encountered a fine

specimen of the *Memphitis Americanus* or American skunk. He was quite disposed to show fight, so Fisher and I opened a lively fire on him with stones, if the bull may be permitted. It was quite exciting to us and very funny to the ladies, as we dodged and ran and threw stones. Finally, we killed him. He had a very fine skin and I was very sorry that its odor prevented us from saving it. I was told afterwards that this could have been done if the animal had been thrown in running water at once. Col. Dodge, in his "Book on the Plains," gives a number of well authenticated instances in the Valley of the Arkansas, where skunks have stolen into camps and bitten people, the bite producing hydrophobia. But I could not learn of any such occurrence in either Montana or Colorado.

That night we made elaborate preparations for our friends, the horse thieves. The horses were picketed close together in the bottom, and Fisher and Horace slept among them, one armed with a revolver and the other with my twelve-bore, loaded with buckshot. Sam slept with his head on the saddles and a revolver close to his hand, and I had my Winchester by my side. It was understood that if any of our party was obliged to move about, he was first to whistle in a certain way, and if he heard or saw any one else who did not whistle as agreed upon, he was to peacefully shoot at him, without asking any questions.

We could now appreciate the intense hatred which is felt on the frontier for a horse thief. To lose our horses where we then were would have placed our party in a terrible plight, and none of us felt the slightest compunction at inflicting summary justice upon any one who might attempt to steal them. At the West, whatever leniency may be extended towards homicide, the penalty of horse stealing is death, inflicted by the captors, without troubling the Courts. Still, horse thieves exist, and are bold and cunning.   We heard of one case where a man who slept with his horse's halter in his hands, awoke to find it cut and his horse gone.

Our men, however, were thoroughly accustomed to this sort of thing, and made their preparations as a matter of course.

As a rule, they slept lightly, and the least stir among the horses would always bring them to their feet. These western horses are almost as good as a dog at detecting the approach of strangers.   If they would hear or smell anything unusual, they would at once stamp and snort.   Our men stated that a horse sleeps twice during the night ; once between eleven and twelve o'clock for about an hour, and then from two to half past three o'clock.   In his first sleep he usually stands, in the second he usually lies down, but not always.   In either case, he awakes and is uneasy at the approach of a stranger.

If, when at home, we had been told by a policeman that burglars were hanging about and that there was a strong probability that the house would be broken open during the night, the sleep of the family would have been brief and troubled.

Although a raid of horse thieves would have been very much more serious in its results to an outfit like ours than any theft of burglars could be at home, yet we had experienced so many queer things during our trip, that it took a good deal to disturb us.   So we went to sleep precisely as usual and slept the sleep of the just, my wife contenting herself with warning her daughter that if she heard guns firing not to sit up, but lie as close to the ground as possible.   Once during the night I thought I heard a noise and got up and looked out.   I did not go out of the tent, for everything seemed all right, and furthermore, I am a poor musician and was not positive that I could whistle the notes agreed upon correctly enough to satisfy a suddenly awakened man.   It was five o'clock when I awoke the second time. The sun was then shining brightly and I went out. The ladies were still sound asleep, and the men, tired out by their vigil which daylight had rendered unnecessary, were sleeping even more soundly, so that I had to call them several times to wake them up. This was another of the occasions when a dog would have proved of value, as his instinct and senses as to the approach of suspicious characters are rarely deceived.

CHAPTER XX.

AN ELK HUNT.

As soon as Fisher was awake, he and I, without waiting for breakfast, started out to reconnoiter for elk, more
to lay our plans for subsequently finding them, than with
the expectation of meeting any that morning. The river
makes a large circle through the valley trending off to
the west. We therefore struck out to the east through
the woods so as to swing around and meet it. It was a
beautiful country. The woods were without underbrush
and open ; the trees being so far apart that except where
there was a windfall, there was little of that climbing
over fallen trees that is found in Eastern forests. We
were constantly passing through little grassy parks, oval
shaped and bordered by groves, just the place to find
game. As we both wore rubber boots and there were
few fallen branches, our footsteps made no noise, and we
walked quite swiftly, keeping a sharp watch for fresh
tracks leading to the river. We found many well beaten
elk trails and old bear "signs," where the bears had torn
a rotten log to pieces so as to get at the ants it contained,
but no fresh tracks of either. When we first started we
only intended to walk a short distance, but we concluded
that it would be just as well to settle the question as to
whether or not there was any game on that side of the
river, and therefore kept on. After walking about three
hours we struck the road and followed that back, watching carefully, as everything that went to the river had to
cross it, and a road so little traveled as this showed the
track of every animal which crossed it much plainer than

the hard ground would have done. We encountered a good many tracks of different kinds, but only two of elk and these were going away from the river and seemed hours old.

By this time the sun was well up in the sky and walking became warm work, the more so as there was no breeze. We were still a long way from camp, so that it was not until ten o'clock that we reached it, tired, hot and hungry with our five hours' walk. I must say that I cannot conscientiously recommend a twelve mile walk before breakfast.

During the day we rested in camp, while the men crossed the river and reconnoitered the other side. They found plenty of tracks leading to the mountains beyond, and I decided to try my fortunes in that direction in the morning. I intended at first to take one of the horses as a pack-horse, to bring back anything that I might kill, and the men got a saddle ready. Being far from confident of getting any game, I finally concluded that Fisher's horse and mine would carry all the meat we would be likely to get, and that the annoyance of leading a pack-horse through the woods would more than counterbalance any advantage resulting from having him. I therefore gave up the idea and decided to only take our two riding horses, our blankets, and as little else as possible. Subsequent events proved this was a mistake, as the pack-horse would have saved us much trouble. I made another mistake, also, in not seeing myself just what we were taking. It should be an inflexible rule for every sportsman to personally see that everything which is required on a trip is packed.

Early in the morning Fisher and I started. I had a double blanket rolled up and tied to the cantle of my saddle, in which was an extra pair of heavy drawers and stockings and a knit jacket, and my rubber coat was tied to the pommel. Fisher had a can of corned beef and half a loaf of bread rolled in his blanket. This was our entire outfit for a two days' trip. I carried my Winchester and a belt full of cartridges, and he had the 22-caliber rifle for birds, if we met any. Crossing the river we soon struck several elk trails, as well beaten as a foot-path, leading directly to the mountains. Following them over the ridge back of the river, we now reached what had once been a series of beautiful parks. Fire, however, had run through them and destroyed every green thing. The trees were white skeletons, and the ground hard and bare, making it a picture of desolation. It was also a difficult country to find one's way in, as one park was precisely like another, and the trees were just thick enough to conceal the surrounding mountains. We had ridden about an hour when Fisher suddenly stopped and held up his hand. At that moment four antelopes emerged from the trees some four hundred yards to my left. They did not seem to see us, but leaped and bounded as if in play, running in a circle. I jumped off my horse and got my rifle ready, but they were then six hundred yards off and going like swallows through the air, and it was useless to shoot. I have heard friends describe how they kill running antelope at six hundred yards, but I know I cannot perform such a feat, and therefore prefer to save my ammunition for something I feel I have a reasonable chance of hitting.

It was beautiful, however, to watch these graceful creatures as they sailed along over fallen trees and scarcely seemed to touch the earth in their flight.

Game of all kinds is a curious thing, and is often found in the most unlikely places. But I confess my inability to understand what antelope were doing in that burnt-over country, where there was not a spear of grass or a green thing, nor a drop of water within ten miles. It was a good cover for them, however. Their forms blended with the dead trees so that it was almost impossible to see them except when they moved, while they could observe everything around them for a great distance. Besides, the ground was so hard as to make it very difficult to follow their tracks. Perhaps these were the reasons which led them to resort to so unattractive a region.

Antelope are unlike other game in not seeming to care whether they are seen or not. Their large bulging eyes give them a wonderful power of vision, and they always select a haunt which enables them to observe everything that approaches them, trusting to their speed for safety. This is so great that ten or twenty miles is nothing to them, a fact which explains why they are found so far from water.

The sight of these antelope at once put us on the alert. We had no time to regularly hunt for them, even if the ground had been such as to make it advisable, but nevertheless, we kept up a vigilant watch around us as we rode along. This vigilance is also the habit of the antelope; and as his life depends upon it, he naturally keeps a brighter lookout than is the case with one who only depends upon it for his dinner. Consequently, we were not surprised some hours later to see half a dozen more antelope suddenly start out from a patch of burnt timber 500 yards ahead of us, where there had not apparently been the slightest sign of their presence, and flit off among the trees like startled ghosts, with a swiftness which rendered shooting them mere folly.

About three hours after leaving camp we reached the foot hills. The first were low and burned over, but finally, to our great relief we emerged from the burned district and found ourselves once more among green vegetation. After a little reconnoitering we found a large runway, evidently made by elk in going from the river to the mountains. It was as broad and hard as a well used foot path, and wound around the knolls and over the slopes at the easiest places. Animals as a rule always select the easiest paths, and a sportsman in climbing in a strange country will find it better to follow a well defined runway than to attempt to select a road for himself. We now proceeded with as much caution as was possible to exercise on horseback, for we could see recent fresh tracks of several large elk, in or near the path over which we were riding. But as we reached the top of one of the hills and started down into the little valley between it and the hill opposite, a current of wind blew freshly from behind us. At almost the same instant we heard the sharp snapping of a twig and a dull "bump," "bump" below us. On proceeding a few yards further we found the explanation, though but little explanation was needed to a hunter of any experience. In the trail and near it were fresh hoof marks as large as those of a horse, the tracks of several elk, by which it could be seen plainly where they had leaped and then dashed off at the top of their speed when our scent reached their sensitive nostrils.

"I have heard a good deal of talk about hunting game on horseback," remarked Fisher, "but I am darned if *I* ever saw anyone work up to anything in that way, and I never expect to either."

Crossing a brook we were now in a little cañon at the foot of the mountains which line the base of the bare and snow-clad peaks. The Rocky Mountains rarely, if ever, rise directly from a plain, but extend in hill behind hill, and mountain behind mountain, each higher than the other, the last being known as the "peak." Each hill and mountain is separated by cañons of greater or less depth, so that hours of climbing are required to reach the foot of peaks that seem close at hand. We were now in a beautiful little valley, hemmed in on one side by the hills we had just surmounted, and on the other by the steep side of a high mountain from which fire and storm had cleared the timber, or piled it into slashes or wind-

rows. As the grazing and water were good, we determined to camp there. Saddles were ungirthed, the horses
picketed with great care, and after a hasty lunch we set
out to climb the mountain " still hunting " for elk. The
prospects to me, at least, did not appear bright. The
wind was directly behind us blowing in gusts, rendering
it certain that we could not approach any game from our
side of the mountain without alarming it, even if the
ground had afforded sufficient cover. We therefore had
to make a detour and ascend the mountain from the other
side. Beside the wrong direction of the wind, there
were any quantity of dead twigs and small branches hidden in the grass, which when stepped on, snapped with a
noise which sounded, in the stillness of the woods, like
the report of a pistol. The course we took was diagonal,
around and up the mountain. As we rounded it we found
many more trees than on the side towards our camp. The
timber was, however, open and interspersed with little
grassy glades. It was about ten o'clock in the morning
when we left the horses, and all the afternoon we climbed
and scrambled, stepping like cats over fallen trees, dodging through projecting limbs and doing our best to move
with the utmost silence. Finally, we found a large and
well frequented runway which was a great assistance, both
because it followed an easy grade and because we could
walk in it in silence. We were now fully nine thousand
feet above the sea, and although I had become somewhat
accustomed to the rarified air, the ascent was difficult, and
I had very frequently to stop to rest for sheer lack of
breath. The sun was also hot; and the heat added to
the difficulty of breathing, made the climbing no child's
play. Yet the air was so bracing that after a few moments
rest in the shade all sense of fatigue disappeared. Here
we encountered, for the first time, some true pines, magnificent trees fully four feet thick at the butt, towering
far upward and casting more shade than a forest of the

bull pines to which we had been accustomed for so long, would have done. It is impossible to describe how grand they appeared to be to us after our long association with the spare foliage of the latter, and how grateful it was to stretch one's self in their shade, and while regaining our breath, admire the magnificent scenery that each upward step opened to our view.

Finally, we reached the shoulder of the mountain and, as we feared, we found ourselves on the edge of a broad and deep cañon which separated the mountain we were on from the main peak. Although we were now almost up to timber line, if we desired to scale the peak itself it would be necessary to descend into this cañon and ascend on the other side, and even after reaching our present altitude, there would be the rocky peak itself to surmount, to do all of which would require fully three days of tough climbing.   At first it seemed as if we would have to do this ; as the main herd of elk and particularly the bulls, as is their habit in summer, had gone into the lofty peaks above timber line to avoid the flies.

The prospect was one of grandeur, however unpleasant to a sportsman.   At our feet was a precipitous cañon, its frowning sides fringed with pines which seemed to dwindle into shrubs at its base.   Beyond this, and just opposite, at the distance of about a mile, arose the majestic mountain top, forming the backbone of the range. Its steep sides were covered with timber for a few hundred feet above where we stood, then appeared sparse patches of vegetation, and above these a vast expanse of bare and precipitous granite, so ruddy that it was almost pink in the rays of the Western sun, except where the snow banks in the ravines and clefts relieved it with great patches of glittering white.   All around us, as far as the eye could reach, were other rocky and snow-clad peaks, among which none but the hunter or hardy prospector had ever penetrated.   Yet those who had the muscle and nerve to penetrate their recesses would find a hunter's paradise ; for this was the home of elk, mountain sheep, grizzly and cinnamon bear. Whether or not we would have to attempt the ascent of this peak depended upon our being able to find any game in the mountain over which we were climbing, and we determined to hunt it with the greatest care.

Right on the edge of the cañon, and in a little "cooley" some fifteen deep we found a beautiful cool spring, the first we had met during the day, and seldom did water taste better than it did to our parched throats. Refreshed by this, we skirted silently along the edge of the cañon until nearly opposite our camp, and then, facing in that direction began to climb towards the summit.

Our hopes of meeting game were greatly dampened as we continued the ascent. Although we had swung completely around it, the wind seemed to shift and still blew from behind, warning all game of our approach. Soon we entered a tangle of fallen timber, through which it was impossible to penetrate in silence. As one of us stepped off a log into what looked like a clear space, his foot came upon a dead limb concealed by the grass, which snapped with a sharp "crack." Instantly, like an echo, came a "snap," "crack," "crack," followed by a dull "bump" "bump," from just in front of us. We exchanged looks which spoke volumes.

"There he goes," said Fisher, "scaring every ——— thing ahead of us."

For myself, my disgust was too deep for utterance, for our slender chances for sport seemed to vanish with the retreating elk.

Climbing becomes hard work when your judgment tells you it will be barren of results. At about five o'clock we finally reached the foot of the crag that formed the mountain summit. Passing around the left of this, we emerged upon the bare slope at its base and halted ; I sank down upon a log breathless, tired out and disgusted, and even Fisher, accustomed as he was to mountain-climbing, was glad to imitate my example. After resting for a few moments Fisher took my glass and carefully examined the slopes of the surrounding mountains. Every dark object, rock, and little bunch of timber was carefully scrutinized, but nothing was seen. Just as I was returning the glass to my pocket, Fisher grasped my arm violently and whispered with great excitement :

"Don't move, there they are. To think of my being such a fool as to be looking half a mile off, when they are right under my nose down there in that burnt timber."

Sure enough, in a broad maze of fallen logs, a sort of windfall to our right and below us, which we had hitherto entirely overlooked, were to be seen several shining hides and an occasional movement. They were elk, four hundred yards off and a hundred yards below, with their heads down and slowly feeding away from us. From where we were, the ground sloped towards them at an angle of thirty degrees, without a rock or shrub to serve as cover.

"It's too far to risk a shot," said Fisher ; "we must cut around the peak and head them off."

Crouching as low as possible, and in a state of suppressed excitement, we softly stole around the summit of the peak and then started on a hard run.

When I sat down, three minutes before, I was so tired and out of breath that it seemed as if I could not move another step. Even when fresh, a three minute run at that altitude would have rendered me helpless, like most "tender feet," until I could regain my breath. Yet, under excitement like the present, all sense of fatigue disappeared, and my breath was restored like magic.

For a quarter of a mile, over rocks and loose boulders,

we ran at the top of our speed, keeping sufficiently below the summit to conceal our movements. Then we stopped, and Fisher, crawling up on his hands and knees, peeped cautiously over the peak, took a hasty view, and then slid back.

"It's all right—let's run for that notch, and we've got 'em."

Another dash of a few minutes, and at headlong speed, and we came opposite a little depression in the mountain toward which the elk were feeding. Casting our hats on the ground (which should always be done in looking at game over a ridge) we crept up softly and peered over. Everything was propitious. The wind blew strong in our faces, carrying away our scent and the noise of our approach, and the elk were unconscious of our presence.

It is a singular fact that during periods of the greatest excitement, when all one's faculties are apparently concentrated upon a single engrossing object, the mind receives and retains vivid impressions of the surrounding circumstances. The keenest sportsman could not have been unmindful of the superb beauty and majestic grandeur of the prospect that lay before us, from the peak on which we stood, and it made an impression upon my mind that I shall never forget. Below us spread a vast panorama. The mountain sloped sharply downward with an abrupt descent, its sides spotted with clumps of fallen logs, interspersed with bare ridges and scanty patches of grass. From its base extended the foot-hills, clothed with timber, one rising behind the other in apparently endless succession, until they melted into a broad valley, which extended for miles until it reached the rocky and snow-clad peaks which formed its further boundaries. The sides of the steep mountain, the numberless hills, the broad valley and the peaks beyond, all lay before us like a magnificent picture.

But the beauty of the scene did not cause us to forget our game.

The edge of the fallen timber in which the elk were feeding was about a hundred and fifty yards distant from us, and some fifty feet below. No elk were to be seen. Nothing but a large reddish spot among some fallen logs, which might well be taken for a rock.

Stepping up, so as to get a clear view over the summit, I dropped on one knee and softly cocked my Winchester.

"Steady," said Fisher, "wait till he comes out, and remember it's down hill."

An instant's pause, then the reddish spot moved, a head quickly appeared over the timber and as quickly disappeared, and then an elk as large as a horse emerged out into an opening in full view, not looking at all as an elk is represented in pictures, but awkward in movement, with back humped up and head down like an old cow, as most game appears when not alarmed or excited.

The severe exertions of the last few minutes were far from being conducive to good shooting. Every muscle was trembling, and my lungs were panting like a blacksmith's bellows. Yet, as the elk appeared, the power to control tremulous muscles and shaky nerves, born from the experiences of many exciting rifle matches, again returned, and as I braced myself to shoot, they became as steady as if I were once more shooting on a team at Creedmoor.

Thinking to myself, as a rifleman does when aiming, "It's a hundred and fifty yards, but down hill—fine sight and low down," I drew the Freund sight of my rifle so that its bead was just visible above the division in the rear sight,[*] aligned the glittering bead close to the fore-shoulder of the elk and just above the lower line of his body and gently pressed the trigger, and then, quick as lightning, threw another cartridge from the magazine into the rifle barrel. At the report, the clumsy animal

---

[*] See reference to sights, on page 40.

below gave a tremendous leap in the air, and for the first time, looked as elks are drawn in pictures. But the Keene bullet had penetrated his vitals, and when he struck the ground it was to fall all in a confused heap, dead as a door nail.

The sharp crack of the rifle and its deadly result was followed by a scene of wild excitement and confusion. Three other elk whom I had not previously seen, a cow and two yearlings, started up from where they had been crouched among the timber and rushed panic stricken in different directions at the top of their speed, two to the left and one to the right, leaping over the fallen tree trunks with surprising agilty for such large animals.

Swinging my rifle around so as to cover the fore-shoulder of the cow, and aiming a little ahead, I pulled the trigger. At the report she fell headlong, but regained her feet and was making a frantic endeavor to scramble over a high log, when another shot laid her prostrate across it.

Aiming a foot ahead of the yearling, to allow for the speed at which he was running, I fired a fourth time. But just as I pressed the trigger he wheeled and ran at right angles, so that I shot ahead of him. He then ran around a little grove until he reached a place just high enough to conceal his body and yet enable him to look over. Here, supposing he was hidden, he stopped, as deer will do, and looked back to see what had caused such extraordinary noises, for probably he had not caught sight of us as yet. I could see nothing but his head, appearing just above the brush, and it was a small mark to hit at such a distance (fully two hundred yards). Taking steady aim between his eyes I pulled the trigger. The bullet struck him exactly where I aimed, and he fell in his tracks as if struck by a sledge hammer, every limb seeming to give way at once.

All this time Fisher stood by my side wild with excitement, yelling :

"That's it—that's it, knock 'em down, knock 'em down !"

He now exclaimed :

"There's the other feller going over the hill—shoot quick !"

Swinging around to the right, I saw the last yearling was bounding up the peak, and fired at him just as he reached the summit. The first shot struck him in the shoulder and whirled him around, and a second, an instant after, and the last in my magazine, tumbled him also to the ground. This made four elk killed in seven shots, with only one miss, the whole occurrence, though seeming to consume a long time, probably not actually occupying half a minute.

This was indeed sport, and more than repaid for all the fatigues and trials of the day, and Fisher and I then and there celebrated the occasion by a "nip," which, however, had to be moderate, as our supply of whiskey was limited to the contents of a half pint flask.

On viewing the dead elk I was surprised at their size. The two large ones were as big as an ordinary horse, and the yearlings were half their size, and I began then to regret having shot so many.

Throughout the trip I had constantly preached against killing any game, or catching fish that were not needed for food, and I had hitherto lived up to what I preached as every sportsman should. Sam had once remarked to my wife in his quaint way : "The General talks a great deal about killing game that is not needed ; but I should just like to see him turn his old Winchester loose among a band of elk, and if he stops, as long as he has a cartridge left, I will eat my hat."

And it is a fact, that no matter how one may theorize, it is practically impossible during the rush and excitement of an encounter like this to stop to think, and the sportsman who can refrain from firing when a good shot at large game is suddenly presented, deserves to be stuffed and placed on exhibition.

This was the first opportunity I ever had of testing the Keene bullets on large game, and I was surprised in cutting up the elk at their destructive effect. In the second elk that I had shot, the bullet had struck a rib (the third, I think), which was nearly an inch thick, passed through it, making a hole in its reverse side two inches in diameter, cut a hole through the lungs large enough to admit the hand, and passed completely through the opposite rib. We picked it out between the rib and hide, and found that it had spread into a four-pointed star and had lost only one of its points in penetrating so much of solid bone and flesh. The ball that struck the yearling had hit him between his eyes, and had taken off the entire top of his skull back to between his ears, leaving a hole large enough to admit one's clenched fist. Fisher said that when the bullet struck, he saw the pieces of skull fly into the air like chips from a log.

My own judgment is, that for killing large game the Keene bullet is superior to the Express, as giving nearly as great a shock and very much greater penetration, and consequently a paralyzing effect, while it can be shot at much longer distances. Its trajectory, however, like that of any solid bullet, is much higher than that of an Express, which involves the necessity of much more calculation, being made as to the distance and guessing as to the necessary elevation.*

Now that we had secured the game for which we had come so far, we began to realize that what to do with it was a serious question. We were on a projecting spur of the mountain, at least 2,000 feet above our camp. There was no path, and the mountain side was as steep as a gable-roof, and was intersected with windfalls where the

---

* See remarks on rifles, on page 232.

trees were so locked together as to make it difficult for a
man to get through, much more for a horse. We had
only two horses; these were cayuses, which had not
" packed " any game, or anything else, in fact, that year.
The probabilities were that they would be frightened by
the smell of fresh meat, and the place where we then
were was about the worst that could be devised to manage
a frightened horse. The immediate thing to be done,
however, was to dress our game, and not to borrow
trouble, so we went at this indispensable but disagreeable
task. While butchering our game, a heavy bank of
clouds came rolling over the mountains at the opposite
side of the valley, and the air became chilly. From the
height where we stood 'it was really a' magnificent sight
to watch these dark clouds sweeping onward to the ac-
companiment of muffled thunder, although our appreciation of it was somewhat reduced by the knowledge that
it involved a thorough drenching. But to our great relief the storm separated just before reaching us, and
passed away over the ranges at each side, where we could
trace its progress by the new fallen snow on the tops of
the mountain peaks.

As soon as the storm had passed, we started for our
camp, each carrying a hindquarter of one of the yearlings. These were larger than an ordinary ham. The
one I carried was not particularly light in the beginning,
and apparently weighed over a ton at the end of our
tramp. The descent was a new experience. We proceeded directly down the mountain, except where our
way was so obstructed by such a tangle of fallen timber
that we were compelled to go around. For a long part
of the way the slope was so steep, that I let the hindquarter that I carried trail along the ground (hide side
down), finding that the easiest way of transporting it.
Sometimes half sliding and half walking, then clamber-
ing over logs, or balancing ourselves along the trunks of

fallen trees, then skirting the crumbling edge of a cañon, we worked our way downwards. Finally, we reached the brook that ran past our camp just about dusk, and for the second time that afternoon enjoyed that greatest of luxuries to a tired and heated man, a drink of pure, cool, water.

A short walk further and we were rejoiced to see our saddles and blankets where we had left them ; but on reaching the spot we were almost paralyzed to find that while *they* were all right, *our horses* were gone ! Think of that, ye dwellers in cities ; fourteen miles from camp, night coming on fast, four elk up on the mountain to handle, and no horses ! They had been picketed in the usual way by a cross rope from neck to neck, and the picket rope attached to its centre. Something, perhaps a bear, had frightened them so that both had jumped at once and broken the picket-rope. In that fading light no time was to be lost, so we started at once after them, the dangling remnant of the picket-rope making a trail which was quite distinct. To our relief, we found them at the lower edge of the cañon, the rope having so caught in a stump, that they had not been able to extricate it. They were nervous from their previous fright, and the smell of the blood with which our hands were plentifully smeared, seemed to render them almost frantic. It was some time before they would recognize even Fisher, or allow him to go near them, and we had " a regular circus " before we could disentangle their picket rope from the stump. At last, however, we got them under control and disentangled, and led them back and picketed them.

While Fisher was doing this, I started a fire and we proceeded to get supper. This was the most primitive meal I had indulged in for many years. By a blunder, caused from giving up taking the pack horse, we had not brought either salt, or butter. In fact, we had nothing

but bread, corned beef and the tenderloin of one of the
elk, which Fisher had brought down in his pocket. Both,
however, had "roughed it" before, and besides, like the
ship-wrecked Irishman, who said "he had a thirst on him
that money would not buy,"we had appetites that
made nothing of such little drawbacks as the want of
salt or butter. Cutting the tenderloin into little strips,
we impaled them on sticks stuck upright in front of the
fire. These, when cooked, we sprinkled with gunpowder
from a cartridge, and used the fat parts of the corned
meat on our bread. For a water pitcher we used the
envelope of my gossamer rubber overcoat, and the bottom
of my flask for a glass. Each had his pocket knife, his
fingers for a fork, and nothing for a plate. The meat
was tender and juicy, and I often wish I could now relish
my dinner at home half as much as I did that rude and
semi-savage repast. And, oh ! the blissful comfort, after
we could eat no more, of sprawling at full length on our
blankets, enjoying a quiet pipe and talking over the experiences of the day. We had swung around the trunks
of two small fallen trees, so as to bring them parallel and
close together, and built a fire between them which soon
made a camp fire fifteen feet long, which kept off the
chill of the night air and threw a ruddy glow over our
surroundings. Beyond its circle of light all was impen-
etrable blackness, except that occasionally, as the fire
blazed up, we could see the shadowy outlines of the
horses.

Our only anxiety was how we should manage with the
horses the next day. If they were so afraid of the mere
smell of blood from our hands, how would they act when
they smelled the blood and carcasses of the elk themselves, and how could we manage them on that mountain
side if they were to undertake to "buck" ? Finally, I
had a "brilliancy," which was to put one of the hind-
quarters of the elk near where the horses were picketed,

but within the firelight, and leave it. The plan worked like a charm. At first, the animals stamped and snorted and made little rushes as far away from it as their picket rope would allow. Then, seeing that it did not move, they drew closer to it by degrees, smelled it with many sniffs, and before long paid no attention to it. As soon as the horses were quiet we turned in. We had only two blankets, instead of the four I had been accustomed to, but our fire was a famous one and made up for our lack of coverings. I kept my rifle by my side, so as to be prepared in case a bear would wander into the cañon during the night, but I should not have heard forty bears, if they had come. I remember laying down my pipe and rolling over—nothing more until broad daylight.

After a hasty breakfast, similar to our dinner of the night before, we mounted and rode up the mountain, zigzagging wherever it was too steep to ascend directly. Soon, riding became impossible, and we had to dismount and lead the horses. They could climb as well as we could—perhaps better, and went like lambs, or to speak more accurately, like goats. It was wonderful to see them scramble over the slopes, wind in and out among the jagged stumps, and get over the fallen logs. I found traveling much easier than on the previous day, partly, I presume, because I was fresher, but more, I think, because my lungs were becoming accustomed to the rarified air. After nearly two hours climb, we reached our elk. I had half expected to find a grizzly among the carcasses, attracted by their scent, but they were untouched. To our great delight, the horses were not in the least afraid of them. As a matter of precaution, however, we blindfolded the former and then hoisted the saddles of the large elk into our Mexican saddles, put those of the yearlings on top, and tied all hard and fast with the picket ropes, for it would not do to have the loads shift. This was not an easy thing to do, as it took our combined

strength to lift one of the large saddles from the ground.
When once in place, however, they were easily adjusted.
Now, we bitterly regretted not having another horse with
a pack-saddle, for the want of which we were compelled
to leave the rest of the meat behind. I then and there
registered a mental vow never again to allow myself to
shoot so much game at once. Our trips up and down
the mountain had so familiarized us with it that the
descent was comparatively easy, and we reached our little
camp with much less trouble than I had expected. As
soon as we had rolled up and tied our blankets, taken a
last farewell drink from the brook and poured some water
around the embers of the fire to prevent its spreading,
we took up our march for our main camp, now fourteen
miles distant.

For the first few miles, while our route lay over the
foot-hills, the scenery was fine and the journey pleasant.
At one time we met a "wood pheasant" (dusky grouse),
a beautiful bird, larger than a partridge, with feathers of
a brilliant peacock blue, walking across our route, as is
the wont of this solitary bird. It did not appear to be in
the least afraid and allowed me to come within fifty feet
of it, but as we had as much, if not more meat than we
could use, I would not shoot it. After we left the hills
and plunged into the burnt woods the journey became
tiresome in the extreme. The horses were heavily loaded,
and that, too, with a dead, unchanging weight, which
was much more trying than that of a rider would have
been. It was hot and close, and there was rarely any
wind, except in the openings. The interminable succession of dead trees and parks was dispiriting; and to add
to our physical discomfort, walking in rubber boots in
the hot sun, began to make our feet sore. We were glad
enough when the sky began to cloud over, even though
it might result in rain. But when the sun became ob-
scured, we could only find our way by the compass, as

all landmarks were hidden by the woods. Suddenly Fisher stopped, and pointing, exclaimes :

"Just see that antelope !"

And there among a few burned trees, within a hundred yards of us, was a large antelope, standing perfectly still and gazing upon us, his figure blending in with the dead trees about him, so that it took a practiced eye to distinguish him from the surrounding objects.

"Oh," I replied," we don't want him, we have more meat now than we know what to do with."

Yet, as the antelope stood and gazed, presenting a mark that would delight the heart of any hunter, my good resolutions not to shoot anything more commenced to ooze out of my finger ends, and I began to consider whether I did not want his head as a trophy. Having decided that I did, I was on the point of taking my rifle from the saddle, when the antelope, with great good judgment, removed from me all temptation to do wrong by departing incontinently and with great speed.

We took a short rest and dry lunch in the midst of this desert and then resumed our journey ; and finally, about three o'clock, reached the Madison at a point about a mile below our camp, which was very straight going through those pathless woods, with nothing but a compass to guide us. It is needless to say that we were warmly welcomed, and that as soon as we had absorbed a quart bottle of beer apiece (which tasted like nectar), we lost no time in exchanging our rubber boots for something more comfortable, to relieve a series of well developed blisters, which we found had been the result of our hot morning's tramp. No one should ever wear rubber boots for a long walk unless it be through water or mud. For still hunting, they are preferable to leather shoes only because they make no noise and do not slip. But they are hard on the feet. Canvas shoes with stout rubber soles, well put on, are far preferable, and are for that purpose the best foot gear that I know of. I intended to take a pair, but put off procuring them too long, and when I tried, discovered too late that I could not find a pair to fit me as easily as would be necessary for long walks—a piece of carelessness for which I did rigorous penance.

Affairs had gone very quietly in the camp during our absence. The men had watched for our friends, the horse thieves, every night, my wife sleeping with my revolver under her pillow, but nothing had been heard. During the day the ladies had fished, read and sketched. Once, to their great excitement, a fine buck with superb antlers had crossed the river just below the camp and stood in plain sight for some time. Sam had tried to stalk him with the 12-bore and auxiliary rifle barrel, but before he got within range the buck had seen the horses picketed in the bottom and fled.

We had much more meat than our party could consume, and I was anxious to take to our friends at Fort Ellis all that we did not need, an undertaking that involved keeping it for a week. I succeeded in accomplishing this by a method that I had previously practiced in the Adirondacks. We cut out the bones and hung the meat in the sun, enveloping it in a mosquito netting so as to prevent the flies from touching it. The sun soon dried the outside surface, making a hard coating which preserved the meat, so that in that dry climate it would, I think, have kept thirty days instead of ten. While traveling, we carried it in the wagon in a sack, and at each camp took it out and sunned it to prevent its becoming musty. I once kept a haunch of venison perfectly sweet in that way for two weeks, in the Adirondacks, where the climate is much more damp, and there are innumerable blow flies.

Both Fisher and I were decidedly tired by our long tramp, and were content to rest on our laurels for the

rest of the day ; in other words, to " loaf " around camp
and let the others do all the work. That evening we had
a dinner which was indeed a dinner. Broiled trout, roast
elk, potatoes, stewed tomatoes and corn, fresh bread, and
for desert, stewed apples and prunes and canned peaches.
After which we felt at peace with all the world.

The meat of an elk is delicious. Like tender beef,
with a suggestion of the game flavor of the best venison.

CHAPTER XXI.

THE CONTINENTAL DIVIDE AND HENRY'S LAKE.

Leaving camp early the next morning, we enjoyed one of the most beautiful rides we had ever had. We had gotten away from the burnt timber and were getting out of the region of the bull pine. For several miles the road ran along the edge of the river through a succession of small grassy parks, fringed with fine trees, and giving a peaceful, rural effect. Then it took us over a high rolling prairie, which seemed like a cultivated field of grass, then through a divide between two thickly wooded ridges, and along swift and cold trout brooks, half concealed in willow thickets. There was a fine breeze, plenty of shade, and constantly changing scenery; everything in short that was needed to make exercise on horseback agreeable. This day I got the first and only fall that any of our party sustained during the trip. I was riding along a perfectly smooth road, at a fast lope, when my horse's foot struck a round stone on the roadside, which was concealed by overhanging grass, so that he could not see it. He went down like a shot, throwing me over his head. The road was soft, and and neither I nor the horse was hurt in the least, although the ladies, seeing me roll away from him (as one always should do when a horse falls with him, to avoid being kicked), at first were a little alarmed. I did not even injure my rifle that was strapped to the saddle, which was a piece of great good fortune.

Our road now ran through Targees Pass, a gap in the Madison range of mountains, which latter here forms the

Continental Divide. Here, in the afternoon, we reached the summit of the Divide itself. Instead of a steep and rugged cliff, it was a small and gently rounding knoll. But a few feet from the top of it was an ice-cold spring, whose waters ran towards the Pacific, while the brook a hundred feet behind us, emptied towards the Atlantic.

On the way we found two dead porcupines which some idiot had killed and left in the road. They were the largest I had ever seen—as large as an ordinary dog. For some reason I do not understand, the cayuse is mortally afraid of a porcupine. My daughter and myself, who were in front, rode close to these suddenly, and it gave a shock to the nervous system of our horses from which they did not recover during the rest of the trip. To use a slang expression—"it broke them all up." From that day forward, whenever my "Billy" or her "Daisy" (neither of which had ever before shied with us), caught a glimpse of a rock or stump in the outlines of which they thought they could discover the faintest resemblance to a a porcupine, they would shy six feet to one side, as if they had seen a grizzly. Fortunately, we were now so accustomed to the saddle that this trick did no more than annoy us, but this it did most thoroughly. There is nothing more aggravating than when riding quietly along to have your horse go flying sideways out of the road for nothing at all. And yet, punishment will do nothing to cure him.

While riding through the woods of Targees Pass, we suddenly came upon a singular "outfit." First appeared a two-horse wagon, covered with canvas. On the front seat was a man and his wife, the latter holding a very small baby, which sent forth a plaintive but persistent wail. In the back of the wagon was a door, covered with mosquito netting, through which we could see that the floor was covered with mattresses, on which several children were playing, who all rushed to the door to look at us with curiosity similar to our own. This was evidently the family bedroom. Then came another wagon, apparently containing the family goods, and having a stove strapped on the tail board, so that it would be instantly available at a halt. Last of all, on a mustang pony, came a very pretty girl, who rode by with an air of absolute unconsciousness of our presence, which, in these wilds was quite paralizing.

Early in the afternoon we reached the valley of Henry's Lake. The valley is a level prairie, encircled on three sides by high mountains and covered with a thick growth of bunch grass, which had cured as it stood, giving the landscape a dull, yellow color; a hue, which from this time forward was continually before us.

While the curing of the grass detracts greatly from the beauty of the scenery, it is a great aid to the ranchman. All the labor of cutting, spreading and raking hay is avoided. Many lay up no hay at all. Those who do, simply cut the grass and toss it into stacks without any other formality. Stock of all kinds graze upon this grass all the year around, and seem to be as fond of it when dry as if it was green, partially, perhaps, because they have no choice. In the winter the horses paw away the snow which covers it, but cattle have not sufficient intelligence to do this and keep themselves in good condition, and consequently have to be driven out of the mountains before the snow sets in. Bunch grass does not grow nearly as thickly as Eastern grass, but in scattered clumps, which give the impression that there is much less of it than is really the case. But when seen from a distance, so that the stems blend together, it looks like a field of ripe grain which has been stunted in its growth. But in riding over it you find there is no sod, as is the case with buffalo grass and Eastern fields.

Throughout the valley this yellow grass continued in a monotonous, unbroken stretch from the lake which formed its western boundary, as far to the east as the eye could reach. In this latter direction, the view was broken by the majestic forms the Three Tetons, three great conical white peaks, which tower above the level prairie, far from any other mountains, as if three great icebergs had been stranded there. They were seventy miles off, yet the air was so clear that it seemed as if they were within walking distance.

At the entrance into the valley a Mr. Burnside has located a ranch. He had just finished a log-house, made of peeled logs, which was as neat as a pin and quite comfortable. Little Mrs. Burnside was as proud of it as if it had been a Queen Anne cottage at Long Branch. She apologized for its not having a floor. "But the men had been very busy getting up some hay for the winter, and they had to go seventy miles for boards." She had several canaries, a young eagle, a little cinnamon bear, a quantity of chickens, the smallest of French poodles, shaved so as to look as much like a lion as possible, and *Pat*, a brindled bull-dog (that was proudly pointed out as "the Champion of Montana," and looked it every inch), and was just as happy and contented as the day was long. When our tent was up, she made a call on us with her husband and son. The sun was down and our ladies wore their ulsters, but she seemed comfortable in white muslin. She told us that they had come into the valley that spring, and although there was heavy snow for some time after their arrival, they had lived in a tent until recently, when their log-house was ready for use. One of her chickens, she said, made a nest in a snowbank and she had to wade out to it and hold the eggs in her lap, so as to keep them warm until some straw could be put under them. She asked my daughter's age, and when told, said, "Seventeen ! why I had three children before I was seventeen. On the frontier," she said, " women have to have a protector, and they marry early."

She was neat, quite pretty, with gentle manners. The ladies were surprised to see in the front room of the house a stocking-holder, of a pattern which was the "latest agony" in New York. No one could help admiring the pluck and spirits of this little woman, living in this valley, with not three houses within twenty miles, and not a doctor within a hundred.

Henry's Lake is an oblong sheet of water some five miles long by three wide. It is quite shallow and full of aquatic plants, and the brooks which empty into it are so full of beaver dams as to render the shore inaccessible, except in a few places. Its waters swarm with trout and are covered with swan, pelican, geese and ducks, making it a veritable hunter's paradise.

The morning after our arrival we went to the lake to fish. As the boat landing was three miles from our camp we went on horseback. On starting, we were favored with an impromptu circus. "T'other Billy," Fisher's cayuse, had been a little sulky for several days, evidently watching to find his master off his guard, as is said to be the habit of the species when inclined to be "kantankerous." On this morning, the moment Fisher swung his right foot over the saddle to mount, Mr. "Billy" bucked and shied. The movement was so sudden and unexpected that Fisher, although an admirable rider, was carried over to the right, being overbalanced by the weight of my fish basket, which was slung on his right side and contained the lunch for the party, no small weight.

The pony then bolted at the top of his speed. Fisher hung on, Indian fashion, with his left knee over the cantle of the saddle and his left hand at the pommel, making desperate attempts to regain his seat. He would have succeeded, but for the heavy dangling basket. But this made it impossible, and after a short time he was compelled to drop off, fortunately without sustaining any other injury than a wrenched wrist, and away went the

pony over the prairie. Burnside rode after him at full
gallop, and for an hour there was an exciting chase, more
like that of two boys playing "tag" than anything else.
"T'other Billy" would dodge and twist and double, but
at each turn would be promptly headed by Burnside's
horse, which knew his business perfectly, and seemed to
enjoy it. Burnside had no lariat, however, and could
only keep "T'other Billy" circling near us. As soon as
the pursuing horse showed signs of fatigue, Horace
took up the chase on my "Billy." This reinforcement
was too much for the fugitive, who soon surrendered,
but not until after we had been delayed for over an hour.

On the way to the lake we rode by some pack-horses,
which were grazing by the road, and which belonged to
an adjoining camp of freighters. The condition of their
backs was something beyond description. Our men told
us, however, that that was always the case with freighters' animals, as a pack saddle with a heavy load was
almost certain to make sores.

Burnside had a boat on the lake which we hired, and
also procured the services of his man to show us the fishing holes. It is impossible to describe the scorn with
which that old frontiersman looked at my twelve-ounce
split bamboo, (the first fly rod he had ever seen) and the
incredulity with which he asked, "Do you think you
can land a big trout with that?"

It was a poor day for fishing; the sun was bright and
hot, the water still and clear as crystal. The trout were
in the shallow water around the mouths of the brooks
and could plainly see the boat and every motion of the
occupants, so that I had but little hopes of success. As
we approached the first brook I cast my flies, so as to
drop them some twenty-five feet from its mouth. The
moment they touched the water there was a rush and a
great splash, and I had a two-pounder. He made a gallant fight, rushing to one side an then to another, and

then straight away with a force that made the reel fairly "buzz." Our boatman evidently expected at every rush to see the derided rod fly to pieces, but it didn't, and when after many unavailing struggles the trout was finally conducted up to within reach of his landing net, he scooped him in with the subdued remark :

"Well, I'm —— if I thought that you could do it with any such tackle."

Later in the day he admitted "that for *fun*, that is the way to fish."

A landing net was also a curiosity to him, and his method of handling it was at first very original, as he held it in his left hand, took hold of the leader with the right, carefully lifted the trout out of the water and laid him tenderly in the net! Sometimes he varied it by taking hold of the fish instead of the line ; but after a short time he handled it as well as any one could have done. As the water was shallow and the boat crowded, I got out to wade, and had the pleasure of discovering by a cold sensation creep up my leg, that there was a hole in my right wading stocking, a fact that I should have ascertained before leaving home. Shortly afterwards, however, I stumbled and got about a quart of water in the other, so that a fair equilibrium was established between each leg. I had the consolation, however, of finding that the boat frightened the fish away from it so that, even if I was wet I was having by far the best luck of any of the party.

After a while the ladies had become tired with the exertion of throwing a long line, and allowed Sam to use one of their rods. He could flick a fly off any part of his leaders with his long whip, but the use of a fly rod was a new experience to him. After several trials he dryly remarked, "Well, this comes the nearest to throwing nothing, of anything I ever tried."

After fishing for an hour and a half, we stopped, having caught all the trout that our party and the Burnsides could dispose of—besides it was lunch time. The catch was twenty-four, weighing together forty pounds, only one trout being under a pound, which under the circumstances, was as good fishing as could be desired.

After lunch, we rowed across the lake after birds. There were on the water any quantity of ducks and a number of swans, cranes and pelicans. Although they were apparently very tame, they were yet too shy to allow us to come within range. However, I killed several mallards in a little cove, by using Schlieber's thread wound cartridges (which open at ninety yards), and I also got several plover.

After a while the wind sprang up, making the lake so rough as to render it discreet for the occupants of such a heavily ladened boat as ours, to get across it without delay. I was anxious to bag a swan, and in going over, we tried to head off one of those that were swimming along the opposite shore so as to get near enough to try a thread cartridge on him. Several times we approached to within about 200 yards, but whenever we tried to get closer, he would swim a little stronger and shoot ahead of us. Finally he put on a spurt and started rapidly to windward of us. As it was "now or never," I gave Fisher the shot-gun and took my Winchester. Before I was ready to fire, the swan had increased his distance to about 600 yards, so great as to render it practically impossible even in still weather, to hit so small a mark. In a strong wind, and with the boat dancing up and down over the waves, as it was then doing, it appeared to be clearly so. Nevertheless, I aligned the rear sight of my rifle with the fourth bar upon the barrel, which gave the elevation for 600 yards,* and picked out a point about twelve feet ahead of the swan, so as to make that allow-

---

* See method of sighting, page 40.

ance for wind. The boat was so constantly in motion that it was very difficult to level the rifle, and to properly align the foresight upon that point, but after aiming for several seconds, I finally did so and at once fired. I can scarcely say who were the more astounded, myself or my men, to see the swan tumble over and lie outstretched upon the water.

"By George!" exclaimed Sam, that's the best shot that ever was made in Montana." Probably it was, but candor compels me to say that I could not have repeated it, if the prize had been a million dollars, and I had been allowed a week to practice it in.

CHAPTER XXII.

THE CATTLE RANGES.

Starting at 8 o'clock on the morning of August 3rd, our way led us over rolling prairies, the true cattle ranges. After leaving the lake, the hills and prairie we encountered (as was the case with those around it), were all a dull, monotonous yellow. Far up on the mountains on either hand were ragged clumps of timber, forming masses of purple; but with the exception of these, and a narrow fringe of cotton wood along the edges of the river and brooks, like the alders which border Eastern streams, not a tree or shrub was to be seen—not a green thing was visible. Soon we passed over a huge roll in the prairie— really a great hill, if the ascent had not been so gradual that we were hardly conscious of it. This was the Continental Divide, which separates the waters of the Atlantic from those of the Pacific. The slope towards Henry's Lake was well watered and apparently quite fertile. As we rode over it, we flushed a number of prairie chickens, sage hens and other birds, and I could have had fine sport if time had permitted. On the other side of the Divide the scenery was dreary enough. The river ran in a deep cut, concealing the little vegetation which bordered it, and for miles on miles, but for the mountains on either hand, it was like being at sea. The valley had evidently been cut out by the action of water, and appeared to have been the seat of some great lake or glacier. On either side the rise from the present river level to the mountains was composed of a series of terraces, showing the successive banks of the retreating lake. There were usually four of these, rising one above the other, and extending in long regular lines for miles and miles, looking exactly as if they had been formed by a gigantic plane. They were full of water-worn pebbles, which made their sides look like a gravel bed, and which also lay thickly over their surface. The road wound along the base of the second terrace, to take advantage of the earth that had been washed down from it. Yet, the stones protruded through this scanty covering so as to oblige us to walk our horses most of the time, as the fore-feet of the saddle-ponies only were shod, and consequently there was danger of their becoming foot-sore from traveling over a stony road, unless their riders were careful.

All this portion of the country up to the foot-hills was occupied as cattle and horse ranges, and every few miles we would meet with " bunches" of cattle or " bands " of horses. Although some of the bulls had quite a formidable appearance, they seemed to be as quiet as Eastern cattle, and took but little more notice of us as we rode by them than the latter would have done. Still, the appearance of some of these patriarchs of the herd was a little appalling, as they stood close to the trail and faced our passing party, with their shaggy heads held aloft and their fierce eyes glaring at us, occasionally pawing the ground and lashing their sides with their tails.

The cattle did not move in great herds, but were scattered over the prairie and hills in groups of different sizes, "bunches," as they are termed here. These would vary in number from several hundred to five or six individuals, and often a single cow and calf would be met grazing alone. The horses were much more gregarious and generally kept pretty well together. The horses appeared to be mostly bronchos, (*i. e.*, one-third Mustang) and were quite good-sized and well-formed. Some of them were very handsome, although disfigured by the

THE PATRIARCH OF THE HERD.

large brands on their fore-shoulders, with which all were marked.

The subject of brands is one that is but little known in the East. At the West it is a matter of importance, for it is the only method of establishing title to four-footed property. Every stock-owner has his brand, which is regularly recorded, and is well known. It is an immense affair, as large as a frying pan, and is burned into the shoulder of the animal. When the latter changes owners, the seller's brand is vented, *i. e.*, turned upside down and burned on the hip, and the purchaser puts his own brand on the shoulder. Consequently, if an animal is so unlucky as to pass through many hands, he begins to look like a Herald war map.

Every frontiersman always notes the brands upon all the stock that he meets. If you should ask one of them if he had seen a red steer with a white patch on his right eye, branded with a dot in a circle and two notches in his left ear, he would tell you he saw him yesterday forenoon with three other cattle of So and So's herd, at such a place, and you would probably find him there.

We discovered, however, that there are " ways that are dark " on the prairie as well as in cities. It seemed to be generally understood that a promising steer or horse that might find its way into the herd of a ranchman other than its owner would be apt to be found to have acquired a new brand in some mysterious manner.

It was asserted that a hot frying pan placed over an old brand would obliterate it so as to render identification impossible. Croton oil, we were told was also sometimes used for the same purpose, by some cattlemen who did not shrink from stealing another's property.

It was quite a stirring sight to see a band of these half wild horses sweep over the prairie as we rode along; frequently a number of them would stand close to the trail we were following, and watch us with outstretched heads

and then, as we drew near, would gallop around us with
a sweep and rush which forcibly recalled Byron's Mazeppa,
and which made our own horses almost uncontrollable.
On one occasion when, through an oversight, my wife
had been left alone in the rear, her pony was so decidedly
inclined to join one of these circling bands, whose freedom tempted him to forget his duty to his rider, that she
was compelled to call for help, and I had to gallop back
to relieve her dilemma.*   Thereafter we were careful
never to leave either of the ladies alone.

There was a cowboy with some of the bands of horses,
often sitting on the ground in the shade of his horse to
escape the scorching sun, but the others were without
any one to look after them.   The cattle always appeared
to be entirely alone, the cowboys only riding along occasionally to see that matters were all right.

By one o'clock we had ridden eighteen miles, and were
content to halt for lunch at a spring which formed the
watering place of a large ranch.   It was not a pretty
place.   Not a tree or a shrub was in sight.   The roads
were so trodden as to be rough and stony, and the grass
was all gone and the ground worn, giving the appearance
of an entrance to a cattle yard.   The sun was hot and
there was no breeze, so that we were compelled to get out
the small tent for an awning, to protect us while we ate
our lunch.

Up in one corner of the bottom were two weather
beaten tents, in front of which a couple of saddled ponies
stood hitched to a bar.   These were the headquarters of
the cowboys having charge of the range, and none of us
envied them either their occupation or their residence.
There is a certain excitement at times in being on horseback and riding over the country, as there is in being at
sea, but taken on the whole, a cowboy's life is like that

* See Frontispiece.

of a sailor—hard, dull drudgery. It is not surprising that they are apt when reaching civilization to seek relief from the monotony of their lives as sailors do, by a tremendous spree. But cattle owners are more particular now than they used to be, and enforce stricter discipline. Their men are required to be more humane, and there is much less hard drinking and revolver shooting than was at one time permitted ; and the men are getting to be of a better class. One of them rode out as we passed the tents and accompanied us for some distance, chatting upon different matters and giving information about the fords on the river. Travelers on this road are infrequent, and I have no doubt that he was glad to see a new face. He was in the regular cowboy dress (which showed the marks of exposure to the weather), and I noticed he struck his horse at each stride with his big Mexican spurs. This was not so cruel as it seemed, for these spurs are dull and not nearly so severe on a horse as are the small sharp rowels used in the East ; certainly, the pony did not seem to pay the least attention to it. Like all the men I saw of his class, he was quiet and pleasant in his manners, and more than willing to oblige a stranger. In fact, I never saw anybody on the plains, who showed by act or word that he was a ''rough.'' Whether this was because there were ladies in the party, or because we were invariably fortunate in the persons we met, I am unable to say. I can only state the fact as I found it.

When we reached a point where the river turned to the left, he pointed out to me a place where we were to ford it and escape the heavy toll required on the bridge below ; to evade paying unnecessary toll being a cardinal principle in this country. Then with the remark : '' Goodbye, I've got to do down over the bank and look after some calves,'' he swung his pony around on its hind legs with a turn of his wrist, and went over the river bank without slacking his pace in the slightest. The bank was forty feet high, steep, and interspersed with rocks and loose boulders, and at its base was the rapid river. A man on foot would have been obliged to use care in descending. Yet my late companion rode down on a smart lope, his pony jumping over the small rocks and dodging the large ones in a way that made my hair fairly stand on end, although both he and his rider seemed to treat it as a matter of course.

During the ride of that and of several previous days, I had ridden ahead of the party, keeping a sharp lookout for antelope. Only one had been seen, and although that one stood still and stared at us until we were out of sight, he was too far away to be reached. As we were now among the cattle, I had given up the idea of seeing any game, and had allowed the ladies and Fisher to ride some distance ahead of me. Suddenly I heard a cry, and seeing them beckoning to me, I galloped up. To my surprise and disgust, I saw just before them four antelope, which they had almost ridden upon, and which I could easily have shot had I kept in the advance, as I should have done. It was but the work of an instant to dismount and jerk my rifle out of its sling. But the antelope had taken the alarm, and I had the pleasure of seeing them plunge into the brush beside the river just as I was ready to shoot. A moment later, and I saw them scaling the bluff, half a mile in the rear of us. I tried a shot at the "bunch," estimating the distance at eight hundred yards, but it was mere guess work, and I of course missed. These were the last antelope that I saw, and their escape added another to the many lessons which I (like other sportsmen) have received, viz.: "That if you go hunting, you should *hunt all the time;* that your game is most likely to appear where you least expect it, and when you are not prepared for it."

After a ride of twenty-five miles, we made a pleasant camp on a swift, cold brook which empties into the Madison, and the waters of which had developed quite a little grove of cotton wood along its banks. After dinner I went with Fisher down to the river to try for grayling, which are quite abundant in the Madison, but which I had never seen. The distance was not great, but the traveling was the worst I had so far encountered. There were four beaver dams, one behind the other, like regular breastworks, which had to be surmounted. These were overgrown with trees and bushes, and the intermediate space was full of beaver houses and pits, which formed regular man traps and which it would have been very difficult for one to have gotten out of if alone. On reaching the river bank itself, we found it so overgrown with brush that there were only a few places from which a fly could be thrown or where we could get to the water. By the time we got to a suitable place, it was growing so dark that our stay had to be short, for we needed daylight to get back. Our fishing was therefore brief. We caught several grayling, however, of about half a pound in weight ; they took the fly and acted a good deal like trout, and reminded me of the sea trout of Nova Scotia. There were a quantity of grouse in the brush along the beaver dams, and if I had had time I could have shot a number.

The next morning was cold, but we rose early and were on the road before eight o'clock. This day's journey proved to be our first really tedious one. During the greater part of it our route lay along the " bench," the second terrace above the river, skirting the base of the bluff. The road was stony, so that we were compelled to walk our horses, the sun was hot and not a green thing was in sight ; nothing but the sere and yellow prairie and the long lines of bluffs of the same color, as far as the eye could reach. This country was the pathway of the buffalo in their great migrations. Every bank and bluff was seamed and worn by their trails, which wound down their slopes in regular lines, as if they had been ruled. When seen from a distance these diagonal lines on the faces of the long stretch of bluffs looked like the marks of a saw on a rough board. For hour after hour we rode along the foot of these bluffs, hoping as we rounded each projecting spur to see some change in the scenery, and at each turn we were disappointed at finding still another long stretch before us, terminating in a bluff similar to that we had just left. Water, too, was very scarce. About noon we found a cold brook where we stopped for lunch, but after that, did not meet any water until half past five, when we arrived at the place selected for camp. As we had then been over eight hours in the saddle, and had ridden thirty-two miles through a dreary country, we were not inclined to go further. It was therefore with great disgust that we found our proposed camping ground fenced off as a part of the pasture of a large ranch, the broad green fields of which showed that however barren the country might appear, irrigation was all that was necessary to render the valley fertile. While producing plenteous crops, we soon found that irrigation had its drawbacks in producing also an infinite number of horseflies that worried our horses almost into fits, until we had ridden past the wet meadows. The ranchman very kindly permitted us to camp in his pasture, and allow our jaded stock to graze, then charging us only a dollar for the forage of our eight horses. That night we were downright tired, and all agreed that we did not want any more travelling over that sort of country.

The next morning's sun found us rested and invigorated, with the fatigues of the previous day nearly forgotten. Having made an early start, we were delighted to find after a ride of a few hours, that we were leaving the bluffs and emerging upon an open, rolling prairie, where there was a fine breeze, and where a view of the rocky and snow-clad peaks prevented the scenery from being monotonous.

As we surmounted one of the high ridges of the prairie I suddenly saw something like a short-legged dog stealing through the long grass at the base of the knoll on which I was riding. It proved to be a large badger. It was the work of but a moment to dismount and open fire. Why it is that one always over-shoots in firing down hill I confess my inability to explain. But it is an unquestioned fact, and was proved on this occasion. To my astonishment, I missed his badgership cleanly twice at a hundred feet, although using as fine a sight as I could draw (which would have been correct if on a level) and had to hold six inches under at the third shot to hit him. He was quite a formidable brute, with powerful jaws and long curved claws ; he had evidently been in several recent fights, as his hide showed marks of some severe bites. We stopped and took his skin for a foot-rug, as it was quite a handsome pelt. This must be a great place for badgers, or those that are here are very industrious, for their holes were frequent and very large. When I had shot the badger my daughter rode up and sprang quickly from her horse to see what I had shot. Her skirt caught in her saddle, and " Daisy " became frightened and started to run. Fortunately May was able to support herself by the pommel until some one could ride up and extricate her, or there might have been a serious accident.

Soon after we crossed the river and rode into Ennis'. This was a pretty little village plentifully irrigated, and consequently embowered in foliage and, oh! what a relief the sight of this was to us after the monotonous prairie and dreary bluffs over which we had ridden for the last two days. Ennis' rejoices in a store which is surprisingly large and well kept. It was particularly strong in canned goods, as is naturally the case with a frontier establishment. The proprietor, learning that I was from New York, was kind enough to give me a New York " World," containing an account of General Grant's proposed funeral, the first newspaper we had seen in a long time.

While we were waiting at the store, one of the belles of the village rode up on a small but vicious mustang, which she left hitched to a fence while she made her purchases. She wore a short calico dress of no particular style, and a sunbonnet, but she made up for this by a set of enormous hoops. She consequently felt that she was fashionable, and was therefore happy. Soon she emerged from the store carrying a bottle and several brown paper parcels. How she proposed to mount with her arms full, was a problem which interested us greatly. She, however, was not in the least embarrassed. She led her pony to a log, stowed the bottle and parcels in the back of her side-saddle, in such a way that her weight would hold them there, and then with a spring which nearly sent her hoop over her head, and made a most surprising display of under garments, planted herself in the saddle and away went the pony at full gallop, with its rider's hoop showing to the greatest advantage.

Beyond Ennis' the road rises and traverses an extensive plateau. Although this was stony, and the grass apparently very thin, so that it was a wonder how anything but a sheep could pick up a living, several large bands of horses were scattered along it, sometimes as many as five hundred being together, their graceful figures making a great addition to the scene. They were either more shy than the bands we had previously met or else more accustomed to people, for they manifested no particular curiosity at our party, and moved away as we approached. All along the hills which bounded this plateau to the left ran a large irrigation ditch. It was several miles in length and as large as a mill race. If full of water, it would have made the country fertile, but it was as dry as a bone, owing, as we were told, to the fact that the surveyor who built it had made a mistake in

calculating his levels.   Soon after we saw the smoke from
the smelting houses of Virginia City rising from the tops
of the mountains like a gigantic geyser.

We were now thoroughly seasoned to the saddle, and
by starting early made very good time every day, especially when the hardness of the roads was considered.
After a short ride from Ennis' the plateau ceased and the
road entered a series of gulches and cañons, where timber
was growing, springs were frequent, the scenery attractive, and above all, where there were no more stony
roads.

On emerging from these cañons, whose coolness was
grateful and shade refreshing, we came out again on a
prairie, but one showing signs of human habitation.
Large irrigating ditches full of swiftly flowing water,
tilled fields, and even houses began to be encountered,
and soon we reached Meadow Brook, which was almost a
village.

We drew up the wagon close to a little grove by a large
but very muddy irrigating ditch, tied our horses to the
fence and sat down by it for lunch.   Here I read the
account of the preparations for General Grant's funeral
from the "World" I had received at Ennis', which
brought vividly back many thoughts and ideas that had
long been forgotten.

There was no more incongruity between that occasion
and many others that occurred during our trip, but I
shall always remember it.   I was so much interested in
what I read, and the paper referred to the names of so
many persons that I knew, that it brought back home
associations so vividly as to make my present surroundings seem more strange than ever.

While we were lounging along the roadside after our
meal, the ladies resting stretched out on the grass and
the men smoking, an open wagon drove by us.   A nicely
dressed gentleman sat in front, who, Fisher told us, was

the Territorial Judge. Behind him, in a large rocking chair, sat a stylishly dressed lady carrying a black satin parasol fringed with Spanish lace, which painfully reminded the ladies of our party of what they had left behind them for so many days. The Judge gave us a single and apparently rather contemptuous glance, but the lady was too dignified to notice such a hard looking party, and passed by in Oriental splendor, without vouching us a single look.

As soon as we had recovered from this sad blow to our pride, we mounted and set off. We had not ridden completely through the village when our pride had another fall. Just as was passed the open gate of a farm-yard, out dashed a litter of little black pigs right under our horses' feet, with fierce little *whoofs, whoofs.* It was almost as bad as the porcupines, and our horses " went all to pieces." Fred in particular was almost uncontrollable, and it was all my wife could do to prevent his climbing the fence which was on the opposite side of the road. Imagine our feelings, after all our feats of horsemanship on mountain and in cañon, at being stampeded by a litter of small pigs in the streets of the second village we encountered ?

We had intended to ride that afternoon as far as Red Bluff, but in passing through a little cañon some five miles south of it, where there were the remains of an old mining camp, I noticed a weather beaten log house with a sign

"Sulphur Baths—a sure cure for Rheumatism—25 cents."

A place five miles from any occupied house was such a queer situation for public baths, that I determined to camp there and try them, the more so as we had ridden twenty-five miles that day and all sadly needed a bath.

The old "store," belonging to the extinct mining camp still stood with its windows boarded up and a general air of demoralization. There was also an "arrastro,"

with a ditch to conduct the water to it, both in a fair
state of preservation. Also a small log house with a
little garden patch, and the bath-house. These formed
the entire settlement. There were a good many prospecting holes in the bluffs around where miners had
been "coyotting," as Fisher termed it, and the trodden
ground and scanty grass showed the presence of sheep.
Our men told me that an old man who lived like a hermit
in the house, we saw kept up the baths for the accommodation of travelers, although he owned a good deal of
paying quartz and was reputed to be wealthy.

As soon as the tent was pitched I went up to see the
bath-house. It was a log house, built over a hot sulphur
spring. Four wooden boxes, each six feet by four, and a
foot deep, had been sunk in the floor at one side (which
were the bath-tubs), and were separated from each other
by a low partition, giving the effect of stalls in a stable.
Two auger holes, one at each end of each tub and plugged
with sticks, served to let the water in and out, while cold
fresh water was brought in through pump-logs from the
hill above, so that the water in the tubs could be cooled
to any desired temperature. A side door opened upon
the spring itself, a beautiful pool, twenty feet across, and
very hot. The entire place was well scrubbed and kept
as neat as a pin. Towels the size of a handkerchief,
well worn but clean, were hung around, while soap, and
nails on which to hang's one's clothing were provided.

The water was strongly impregnated with sulphur and
as hot as could well be born, and felt delicious to limbs
weary with the saddle. Far different from Bath Lake at
the Mammoth Springs, it left the skin as soft as does a
Turkish bath.

After I had taken my bath, the ladies went up, while I
kept watch to see that they were not disturbed. The
baths were well patronized, for that afternoon, besides
our party, they were used by two passing travelers, and

afterwards by a wagon load of women coming from gracious knows where ! Where the proprietor was we did not know, and therefore to our great regret were unable to pay him. Perhaps his absence accounted for such a rush of business.

In order to cover as great a distance as possible before the heat of the day, we had now adopted the plan of riding off as soon as the tent was struck, leaving the men to pack up and follow us. Consequently, on the next morning, we were on the road by as early as a quarter to seven, and reached Red Bluff soon after. This was the first regular mining camp we had encountered. The first of it that we saw was what should have been the last—the graveyard. If this was a fair sample of Montana cemeteries, it explained why people live so long in that Territory, for no one would submit to be buried there if he could possibly avoid it. It was a sort of goose pasture on the summit of a little knoll, without a fence, and contained about a dozen graves. One tomb was dignified by a rough fence of palings, the others had merely a board at their heads. Fisher looked at it with contempt.

"It can't be much of a camp," he said. "Why, they ought to have a dozen graves started in three weeks if things were anyway brisk."

There was more in this than a joke ; for if the miners were prosperous they would have plenty of money and therefore of whiskey, the drinking of which would lead to quarrels which usually involve shooting somebody— and consequently a full graveyard.

Red Bluff is built in a narrow cañon, and rejoices in a hotel, a store, and two quartz mills built of stone, and about a dozen one-story, flat roofed log cabins, like cow houses. Apparently there had been heavy gaming on the previous night, for the road from the hotel to the store was littered with playing cards. As we rode by, men, usually tall and slim, blue shirted and broad hatted, lounged to the doors and windows (which were all wide open) to look at us. Not a woman or child was to be seen, although we saw the tracks of little bare feet in the road. The inference from the graveyard appeared to be correct. Things did not look thriving; several cabins were empty and one quartz mill was closed.

Beyond Red Bluff the road for several miles runs through a magnificent cañon. The wall are not more than four hundred or five hundred feet high, but are perpendicular, rocky crags, and the passage between them is narrow, and extremely picturesque. After our long ride over the desert and waterless prairie, the coolness of the shady cañon and the sight and sound of the rushing water were inexpressibly grateful. Emerging from this cañon, which we left with regret, we turned to the right and rode over the divide which separates the Madison from the Gallatin Basin. Here, again, was a treeless prairie, only varigated with gophers and gophers' holes innumerable, a sign that Bozeman was not far off. As our ponies climbed over hill after hill, other hills still higher appeared behind them. Finally, as we surmounted one which rose almost to the dignity of a mountain, the valley of the Gallatin lay before us, with Bozeman in the distance, some of its houses glittering like silver. But long before this our horses had begun to whinny to each other, showing that they knew that they were nearing home.

On the way we passed through a sheep ranch. The day was broiling hot, and the herd of over a thousand sheep were huddled into two compact squares, each sheep with his head drooped so as to bring it into the shade of his neighbor, like a chicken with its head under its wing, the flock presenting a most singular appearance. Close to them was their shepherd, a long-bearded, quaint-looking old fellow with an enormous green umbrella over his head and a fine collie dog by his side. We could not help sympathizing with him. To spend one's days sitting and

watching stupid sheep, without seeing a human face or
hearing a voice is maddening ; sheep herders often become insane, and no Western man will accept employ-
ment in that capacity if he can possibly avoid it. " Why
—I'd as soon herd sheep," is a common expression of
aversion.

The ground we were passing over had been recently
traversed by twenty-seven thousand cattle and fifteen
thousand sheep, and they had cleared off the grass as a
prairie fire would have done. Consequently, our saddle
ponies found it almost impossible to get enough to eat,
and we had that morning been obliged to take up their
girths six inches more than we had hitherto done during
our trip. It was a long thirty miles from where we had
started that morning to our camp on the banks of the
Gallatin. Much of the distance had been up hill, and
we were in the saddle for eight and a half hours. The
distance and poor feed told decidedly upon our ponies ;
and mine, during the last two miles, for the first time
during the trip, stumbled, although the road was level,
and showed signs of fatigue. He was a good horse and
had carried me well, and I was very glad to relieve him by
walking the rest of the way.

Eight hours and a half was a long ride, and the ladies
were quite proud of having been able to do it without
serious fatigue.

Our camp was on the banks of the Gallatin near the
toll house. The stream was swift and just the place
where trout should be. I was unable to catch any, however, and was told that they had all been killed by the
sawdust from the mills, a cause which has depopulated
so many other trout streams in all sections of the country.
Nova Scotia is the only place I know of where the law
prohibits sawdust from being thrown into the streams.

In the farm house (which also served as a toll house),
there were two girls, and we were quite interested in see-

ing them go for the cows. In the East this is a prosaic performance, but not so in Montana. The girls first went into the barn-yard and saddled a couple of mustangs. As these were only half broken, the operation took some time. Then, above the fence, we could see the girls' heads rising and falling, as their horses careered around the barn-yard, plunging and bucking. Finally, some one of the children opened the gate and away the two girls went down the road at full gallop, with their long hair streaming behind them, sitting their horses like centaurs. In about an hour they returned with their ponies quite tamed down, driving the cows before them in a decorous manner. Our men told us that these young ladies always broke their own colts, but judging from what we saw, they were either very careless about it, or on this occasion rode some whose education was not completed. These girls were more afraid of strangers than of fractious horses and kept out of sight during our stay, as was apt to be the case with those of the gentler sex we met on the ranches. Sam, who went up to the house for something, insisted that all of them but one "took to the woods" out of the back door, when he approached, and would not return until they found they knew him. This bashfulness among the females of the frontier was different from what had been represented.

It is said that when a young "pilgrim," of an affectionate and inquiring disposition, inquired of one who was familiar with frontier ways, about Montana girls, the reply was:

"Montana girls? What does a tenderfoot like you want to know about Montana girls? It takes a *man* to suit one of them, I tell *you*. I will just tell you a little story which will show you what kind of girls they raise in Montana, and what show a feller like you would have with one of them. There was a girl, awful pretty, but considered delicate for a Montana girl, that was as good as engaged to a cattle man on the Gallatin. Well, this girl climbed up on to a mountain and sat down, to look over the prairie, and think of her own true love, that was punching steers down there. While she was sitting there and half dreaming, a big, thousand-pound grizzly saw this nice, delicate girl and thought she would make an elegant meal. So he comes up behind her and puts his paws around her waist and gives her a tremendous hug ; a hug, sir, which would have crushed a locomotive boiler. Well, sir, this young, delicate girl, that was sitting there dreaming of her absent lover, didn't faint nor scream, but just gently laid her head back on that grizzly's shoulder and softly murmured, 'a little tighter, Sam.' It broke that bear all up, sir, so that he dropped the girl and went right back to his hole and died."

This, however, I am prepared to assert, was a base slander.

One of the most picturesque portions of the ranch where we were stopping, was its cow-house. This was the original "claim shack" of the first settler. Its flat roof was thickly covered with earth, on which grass and flowers had grown two feet high, forming a pleasing contrast to the pale gray of the logs.

In the morning, several of our horses were gone, and I could not blame them. The grazing was wretched, and they were hungry. Their instinct told them that they were near home, so they broke away from their picket ropes and wended their way towards Bozeman. We were then so near the end of our trip that we did not worry over their absence. It was quite severe, however, upon Fisher, who had to walk some six miles before he caught them. It was curious to watch their trail in the road, which was clearly indicated by the dragging cross-rope. It looked as if they could not have gone a hundred yards without the rope's catching upon something. But they managed to prevent this, or if the rope did catch, one of them would walk around the obstruction until he had unwound it.

Fisher having returned with the truants, we drank our last bottle of beer, loaded our wagon, an easy task, for our supplies were almost exhausted, and "saddled up" for the last time. In two hours more we reached the outskirts of Bozeman, and found the explanation of the strange glitter we had observed on the Divide, in the tin plates, formed of old tin cans hammered flat, with which some of the first settlers had covered the roofs and sides of their houses as a substitute for shingles. A few miles before reaching the town we passed through the prairie on which our ponies were kept when at home. There was quite a herd of other horses there who did not seem to understand why their old companions would not rejoin them, as the latter were exceedingly anxious to do. The herd would gallop up to the road and stand until our party got past them, and then all would squeal, kick their heels in the air and dash off at full speed for a few hundred yards to repeat the performance there when we overtook them. They acted like a lot of impudent, idle boys who were teasing some companions who were obliged to work instead of coming out to play. Their example was a great temptation to our ponies. The latter were too tired and hungry to be very restive, but they were quite disposed to be sullen as they found themselves turning their backs upon their comrades and home. All along the outskirts of the village large irrigation ditches were frequent, and their effects were visible in fields of high grain, which showed the capabilities of the soil.

A few moments more in the saddle brought us to the Eastman House and to civilization. I was desirous of riding directly to the hotel, which would have taken us through the main street. This, however, the ladies peremptorily refused to do, so we came up through the back streets as if we had stolen something, instead of in the

RECOGNIZING THEIR OLD COMRADES.

stately procession which would have been suitable. Dismounting at the hotel, we took leave of our ponies with great regret, May cutting off a lock of Daisy's mane as a token of remembrance.

We had been gone just twenty-six days, during which we had ridden over four hundred and sixty miles. We were dusty and travel-stained and as brown as Indians, so altered, in fact, that they did not at first recognize me at the hotel. Not one of us had experienced a sick day, and we were all stronger and in better health than we had ever been before.

After our long trip, civilized garments felt quite embarrassing. This was particularly the case with my wife, as she had gained twelve pounds and found her dresses inconveniently snug.

Having paid a farewell visit to our good friends at Fort Ellis, we packed up, leaving our camp outfit for the benefit of our men. These, by the by, were altered in appearance, even more than we were. Fisher had shaved his beard, greatly changing his looks. Sam, who in camp, was slouchy in the last extreme, when shaved and in "store clothes" was quite a handsome man. Horace, on the other hand, who was quite good looking in camp, was not improved by a high white collar and flaming cravat. They saw us down to the train, and we parted from them with sincere regret, for they were really good fellows.

This was the day of General Grant's funeral. Bozeman is not a large place, but it did itself credit by the way it commemorated the occasion. Business was generally suspended and a quite an imposing procession marched through the main street, consisting of a band, a squad of the Grand Army, two companies of regular cavalry, and two of infantry from Fort Ellis, and "citizens generally." There were services in one of the churches, and the main buildings of the town were draped in mourning, as we

OVER THE PRAIRIES, HOMEWARD BOUND.

found the case to be with those of every city and hamlet between the Rocky Mountains and the Atlantic.

Once on the train we began again to accustom ourselves to collars and cuffs, to avoid lounging, and to pick up again the threads of civilized life.   As we left the prairies and entered Minnesota, and from there onward the trees and verdure were a positive balm to the eye after the sere and monotonous prairies to which we had been so long accustomed.   In fact, the green seemed unnaturally vivid.

We stopped at Niagara, to show it to my daughter and a niece who accompanied us home, but after the scenery we had witnessed, Niagara looked flat and tame.   This is not to be wondered at when it is considered that it is but one-half the height of the Great Fall of the Yellowstone, and that even this appears to be diminished by its greater breadth.

CHAPTER XXIII.

GAME.

Any account of the Yellowstone region would be incomplete which did not give some description of the game of the country, and I shall therefore add a few words upon that subject. As I have previously stated, as far as the Park itself is concerned, all shooting is positively prohibited, and every endeavor is being made by the Superintendent and his assistants to protect the animals which are found in it, except the bears. This protection tends to render it a haven of refuge for elk and similar large game, which are so ruthlessly hunted in the surrounding country. In the winter of 1884–5, quite a band of elk collected near the Mammoth Springs Hotel, and remained there for some months. They were regularly fed by the Superintendent and became quite tame, but unfortunately they were fired on by some hunters and frightened away. They did not, however, leave the Park, and several of them were seen by travelers, from the stages. Mr. Rosendale, of Albany, who went through the Park while I was there, told me that when his stage in passing over the road from the Forks of the Firehole to the Great Cañon, had reached the summit of the Madison Divide, two large elk emerged from the forest and stood upon a projecting point within a hundred yards of the stage, as if on exhibition. The driver stopped and the passengers enjoyed a good look at the rare sight for some minutes. The elk seemed to be quite tame, and when they finally moved away, did so without apparent alarm. A number of others were seen during the summer by other tourists. I have learned that during the winter of 1885–6, some two hundred more elk wintered in the Park, and it is to be hoped that they can be induced to remain there, as they add greatly to its attractions.

Until recently there have been several bands of mountain buffalo in the Park, particularly in what is known as the Hoodoo country, but they were killed or driven off by the miners from the adjoining mining camps. There is undoubtedly much more game in the Park than a passing tourist would suppose to be the case. The travel is along a few roads, from which the instinct of all animals teaches them to keep aloof. But there is a vast area of mountain and forest within the Park limits which is seldom, if ever visited by travelers, and on which game can and undoubtedly does find a home. In the surrounding mountains, particularly of Idaho, and in the Absaroka or Shoshone range, large game, such as elk, deer, bear and mountain sheep, is reasonably plenty. That is to say, that it can be found by hard work, for the day has passed when any large game can be found roaming over the prairies, waiting the arrival of the hunter.

THE BUFFALO.

The great game animal of the plains, the buffalo, may be regarded as extinct. In the great "round up" of 1885, when every valley and mountain of Southern Montana was scoured by a large force of cow boys hunting up the stray cattle, but a single herd, of about thirty buffalo, were found, and they were promptly exterminated. Yet it is but a few years since the buffalo covered the country in herds whose numbers defied computation.

Up to 1830 the buffalo range covered the whole country from Illinois and Missouri to the Rocky Mountains.

This was so reduced by advancing civilization, that in 1876 it was limited to the northern range, including Dakota, Montana and Wyoming, and the Southern, which covered Southern Kansas, Northern Texas and the western part of the Indian Territory. Col. Dodge says that in 1868, for one hundred and twenty miles, along the Kansas Pacific Railroad, he passed through an almost unbroken herd of buffalo, and that during a ride of a hundred miles in 1872, from Fort Dodge to the Indian Territory, buffalo were never out of sight.

When the railroads were extended into the area occupied by these animals, the "skin hunters" made their appearance, and the buffalo were doomed. These men would start out from some point on the railroad with a regular organization, consisting of a hunter, two or three skinners, a cook, a wagon and a few supplies. On arriving in the vicinity of buffalo, they would encamp. The hunters would then crawl up to within fair range of a herd, being careful to keep well to leeward, hide themselves behind a roll in the prairie or in a buffalo wallow, and open fire. They were usually armed with a very heavy rifle, resembling, except in its weight, a Creedmoor, and carrying a heavy charge, which would throw a bullet completely through a buffalo. Selecting an animal, they would shoot it, aiming to strike it behind the shoulder and low down, so as to penetrate the lungs. When hit, the buffalo would start, stagger a little and fall. His companions, neither seeing nor smelling the hunter, would regard the movements of the wounded buffalo with stupid curiosity but without alarm, and would remain where they were until the hunter, firing about a shot a minute, had killed them all. This was called "getting a stand" on a herd. Instances were quite common where fifty to sixty buffalo have been killed at a single stand. When all were killed, the skinners would come up and strip off the hides, the meat being left to waste. The hides were staked out in the sun to dry, and then rolled up and put in the wagon, and as soon as that was filled, the party returned to the railroad, where a spree of a few days dissipated the money that was received for the hides they had procured, and sent the party off again for more.

The number of buffalo that were killed in this way is something incredible.

Col. Dodge, in his book, "The Plains of the Great West," estimates it at a million a year, which is equal to one-half of all the cattle in Great Britain, and gives statistics showing that from 1872 to 1874, four and a half million buffalo were slaughtered, this being exclusive of the hides that were sent to the West and North.

This terrible havoc continued until the buffalo have vanished before it like mist before the morning sun. It has now ceased for the reason that there are no buffalo to kill. In the Dominion of Canada skin hunting is not permitted, and the remnants of the Great Northern herd linger out a brief existence beyond its border. But within the United States the buffalo is almost as extinct as the dodo. Even their bones, which once whitened the prairie, have been gathered up and shipped East to be used in the manufacture of buttons and similar articles. While it is painful to contemplate the extinction of such vast numbers of animals, and also to think of the waste of food which it involved, it is by no means certain that it has been an unmixed evil. It has settled the Indian question, and brought the wandering tribes of the plains into subjection. Moreover, the vast ranges formerly occupied by the buffalo are being rapidly occupied by cattle and horse ranches, and the time will soon arrive, if it has not already come, when a steer or horse will be found in the place formerly occupied by a buffalo, an exchange which will be for the benefit of civilization and national prosperity.

MOUNTAIN BUFFALO.

The bison or mountain buffalo, an animal but little known at the East, still continues to exist. It is smaller and more active than the buffalo of the plains. Its hair is darker and more curly, its humps smaller, its horns shorter and less spreading. Unlike the common buffalo, which is a stupid animal, the bison is wary in the extreme. It inhabits the sides of steep mountains and the recesses of deep cañons, and can only be killed by a practiced hunter and after severe climbing. There are quite a number in the Park and the surrounding mountains and its vicinity, and it is so difficult to kill them that it is probable that they will be able to keep up their struggle for existence for a long time to come.

This animal is said to be an offshoot of the plains buffalo, whose habits have been changed under the Darwinian idea of the survival of the fittest. I do not, however, attach any great weight to this theory. Habits of a race of animals are only changed in the course of generations, and the onslaught of skin hunters which exterminated the buffalo from the prairies, was too sudden and summary to permit them to change their natures. Besides the mountain buffalo existed as they do to-day when the plains were black with the herds of their more stupid cousins, migrating as they had done for ages previously, and as they apparently would continue to do in the future.

ANTELOPE.

There is no more graceful creature to be found than the antelope, and its flight is the veritable poetry of motion. It stands about four feet high, is about five feet long, and weighs about seventy pounds. Its color is a reddish-yellow, with a white rump and legs, and its eyes are large and lustrous. It is found all over the Great

STARTLED ANTELOPE.

Plains of the West, and also among the foot-hills and lower slopes of the mountains, frequented by the black-tailed deer, with which it seems to live harmoniously. It prefers a broad expanse of prairie where it can see in every direction, as it depends more upon its eye-sight for protection than its scent. Its powers of vision are something wonderful, and the hunter must never assume that any antelope that he sees, even with a glass, is not watching his movements. During the summer, antelope feed in the little open parks, which are scattered along the mountain sides. As a rule they avoid the woods, although I met several where the timber had been burned so that it was open and permitted a view of everything that was approaching.

Antelope are usually hunted in the morning and evening. They are then feeding and are easier to approach than in the middle of the day, when they are lying down and watching.

The bane of the antelope is its curiosity. This will often induce it to approach the hunter sufficiently near to afford a shot. They are sometimes lured on to do so by tying a red handkerchief to a ramrod, or even by the hunter's lying on his back and kicking his heels in the air. They all follow their leader like sheep, and will not quit the track they have selected even if it leads them close to the hunter. They can frequently be turned by firing ahead of them, as they will run from the dust made by the bullet striking the ground, seeming to fear this more than the report of the rifle.

Their numbers have greatly diminished as the country has been opened up. In many portions they are almost extinct, and almost everywhere they are wild and shy.

ELK.

The elk is found all through the mountains in the Park and those which surround it. It is the largest of the deer family, and will weigh from 500 to 750 pounds, or even larger. The horns of the bulls are enormous, reaching to the height of a man's shoulder and weighing from sixty to seventy pounds, and it is common to find them lying on the prairie. It is a mystery how an animal of this size can go through the woods with such an obstruction on his head, but he manages to do it, and that too without making any noise. The elk's habits are much like those of the black-tailed deer. From May to July the bulls are high up in the mountains near the snow line, a locality they seek to avoid the mosquitos and flies while they are undergoing the painful operation of having their horns grow. The female is in the lower foot-hills in some thicket of willow or cotton wood taking care of her calves. About the middle of July the calf becomes old enough to take care of itself, and the mother comes out and feeds on the upper foot-hills and lower mountains. By the first part of August, the horns of the bull have attained their full growth and he gets rid of the velvet, as well as sharpens his horns, by rubbing them against a tree or bush. This is one of the signs by which he is found by the hunter, for the motion of the bush against which he is rubbing his head can be seen for a long distance, and the hunter can steal upon him while he is too busily occupied to be on the alert. The elk is very timid, has a quick eye, a keen ear and a wonderful scent, so that it is no easy matter to stalk him. Elks are great travellers, and there is no certainty that because they are heard of as being at a certain place on one day, that they can be found there the next. They always walk in single file, the trail being arranged so as to follow the easiest slopes and leave room enough be-

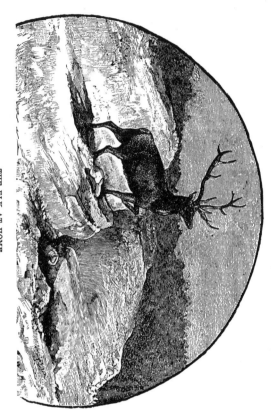

THE ELK AT HOME.

tween the trees so the bulls can pass without striking their antlers, and their trails over the mountains are as well trodden as a path along a village road. The sportsman who encounters a band of them should always endeavor to shoot the front elk. He is the leader, and if he falls, the others will stop and huddle together until another one takes the lead, giving a chance for another shot. The elk is almost as astute as the black-tailed deer in hiding in a small cover or sneaking out of a thicket without any indication of his departure. His usual gait is a trot and he only breaks into a run when hard pressed. His trot is as fast as the pace of a good horse, and his run is but a little faster, and seems to soon exhaust him. Notwithstanding the formidable antlers of the bulls, they are arrant cowards, and instances are very rare of their attacking a hunter, even when cornered or wounded. The bulls will even try to hide themselves among the cows to escape injury.

The most important thing for a sportsman to remember in hunting elk, is always to keep to leeward, as their powers of scent are something incredible. The next, is to avoid making a noise, and the third to move slowly, observe keenly and keep out of sight. In hunting elk as in the case of all other game, great caution must be observed in looking over a ridge. The hunter should take off his hat and lift his head very carefully, just high enough to give him a view of the opposite slope, and should not raise any higher until he is certain that there is no game on the other side which would be disturbed by his presenting himself upon the ridge. He should always carry his rifle low, so that its movement will not be observed, nor any light be reflected from it, as either can be seen for a long distance.

BEARS.

The bears of the Rocky Mountains are the Grizzly, Silver-tip, Cinnamon, Smut-face, Black, and Silk bear. The Hog-back, or real California Grizzly, is one of the largest, most ferocious and dangerous animals on the Continent. The Silver-tip is a little smaller. Its coat of hair is longer and is tipped at the ends with a glistening silvery white. The Cinnamon is of a reddish brown color and is also smaller than the true grizzlies. The Smut-face bear is still smaller than the Cinnamon and has a spotted face. There is very little difference in disposition between all these varieties; the grizzlies and the Smut-face bear are said to be the most meddlesome and pugnacious of the bear family. The grizzly lives in the mountains, but comes down about September, where he is frequently found in the little parks and ravines, feeding on plums, berries and wild fruit, of which he is very fond. He is also a great admirer of ants, and it is common to find old logs which have been torn to pieces by him in searching for them. He is much less dangerous than is generally supposed, and he will always run away if left alone, if he thinks he can do so. If he is wounded, however, or thinks he is "cornered," he attacks his assailants with the utmost ferocity and desperation, and utterly irrespective of their numbers and weapons. The spectacle of an enraged grizzly tearing down upon you with the speed of a horse, roaring at the top of his voice, is appalling. His strength is so immense, his tenacity of life so great, and his disposition, when aroused, to kill his assailant so inflexible, that the average frontiersman is very much disposed to leave him alone. As he says, "he hasn't lost any grizzly," and does not care to hunt for one; and regards with scorn those "tender feet" who do. I have already written something upon this subject at page 42, and I would repeat that no one should attack this bear except when armed with the most powerful rifle, and with some one to support him. He should also be provided with some good dogs who will divert the bear's attention by snapping at his haunches when he makes a rush. When a hunter can steal up to a bear and get a steady shot, a bullet in the forehead or butt of the ear with almost any rifle will produce instant death. But a shot at the head is very uncertain. If the front sight is drawn too coarse, or the animal raises his nose or moves his head when you are in the act of firing, a miss is almost inevitable. If the bullet only makes a flesh wound, the hunter is apt for the first time to appreciate the full force of the expression " as mad as a bear with a sore head." In that case he will want a rifle which will shoot quickly and strike a smashing blow— and will want it badly. While I was in the Rocky Mountains, there was a party there who were hunting for grizzlies, but they were provided with traps of such a size that a large lever was required to open the jaws. These were chained to a heavy log and put in a place where a grizzly would be likely to come. If a grizzly kills any animal, he eats what he wants of it and covers the rest with decayed logs, rubbish or stones, either remaining near the body or returning to it nightly. If the trap is placed in the neighborhood of such a carcass it is very apt to catch him, or the hunter may, if he prefers, conceal himself in the vicinity and shoot him if he comes up. If dogs are used, small dogs who will run around and snap at the animal's haunches are better than those who will attempt to fight. The latter are short lived. I was told of an English gentleman who had two imported boar hounds as large as a man, which he let loose on a grizzly. The first dog jumped at the throat of the bear, who gave him a single hug with his fore-paws, which mashed every bone in his body, and as the second dog jumped past him, the bear dropped the body of the first

IN A SAFE RETREAT.

and struck the second a blow with his fore-paw which broke his back, disposing of both dogs in less than a minute, and if the owner of the dogs had not been fortunate to have several good shots with him, his own chances for life would have been no better than those of his dogs.

BIG-HORNED SHEEP.

The big-horned sheep are quite frequent in the mountains in and around the Park. They are the next animal in size to the elk in this section of the country, being more than twice as large as the domestic sheep, the rams weighing three hundred to three hundred and fifty pounds. To hunt them is very much like the chamois hunting of Switzerland. They live on the jagged peaks of the mountains, among bare and broken rocks, and only descend in the night time for water. The body of the sheep is much like that of the deer. Their color is gray, and the horns of the rams are something tremendous. They make almost a complete circuit around the head, are from two to three feet in length around the curve, and weigh from fifty to sixty pounds. The feet of these sheep are so modelled that they never slip, and they can run up the face of an almost vertical rock, almost as a fly would do. They can only be reached by patient climbing in high altitudes, but when found afford magnificent sport. They are usually found in small bands, feeding on the edges of small meadows, or resting among the high crags of the upper peaks, always choosing a situation which commands an extensive view. In the winter they descend to the lower slopes of the mountains. Their scent is very keen, and they are guided more by that than they are by their sight or ears. If a man passes to windward of them they are off like a bird, running over rocks and precipices over which it would seem impossible for a living animal to pass. They are said to occasionally drop off a precipice and alight upon their horns, a story I do not believe. Their flesh is delicious, particularly in the fall.

ROCKY MOUNTAIN GOAT.

The Rocky Mountain or antelope goat is an animal resembling a very large goat. It has a curious habit of sitting up on its haunches like a bear, when alarmed. Its general habits are the same as the mountain sheep. It is scarcer and even wilder, so that few hunters have ever seen one. It is only to be found in the highest snow-clad peaks, and through great labor. I could not learn that any of them had been seen nearer to the Park than the Bitter Root Mountains.

DEER.

The deer of this section of the country consist of the white-tailed or Virginian deer, which is common in nearly all the States of the Union, and the black-tailed or mule deer. The former frequent the timbered valleys and foot-hills, and are more shy and less migratory than the black-tail. The black-tailed deer is essentially a mountain animal. It is usually found in the broken foot-hills, among the openings in the lower slopes of the mountains. It is of a dark gray or mouse color with very long ears and a thin tail, and is larger than the white-tailed deer, the bucks frequently weighing two hundred and fifty pounds. Its gait is very singular, as it springs with all four legs at the same time, making in its progress a series of jumps or bounds like a rubber ball, and rendering it an extremely difficult mark for the hunter. This gait, however, does not prevent its being extremely fleet and it gets over rock, broken ground and fallen trees with almost the speed of an antelope. The buck loses his horns in February and by May is found along the snow line of the mountains, awaiting the growing of another pair, so that from May to July he can only be found in that vicinity. While the does are not with the bucks during this period, but are taking care of the fawns, they are also well up on the sides of the mountains. In July, the bucks and does both collect in herds, but it is not until October that both sexes congregate together. By this time the horns of the bucks are out of the velvet, and they are constantly fighting. During August and September the approach of cold weather drives the black-tails down from the mountain, and they wander over the country selecting some sheltered place for their winter home. They are migratory in their habits, and frequenty pass over long distances. The black-tail may be found early in the morning feeding in the little glades and openings on the mountain slopes. He then lies down at some place either on the edge of a cañon, where he can see all that is approaching him, or on a point covered by timber. In either case, he is very difficult to bag. He is constantly on the alert, and besides his form blends with the surrounding objects, so that it is almost impossible to see him, and the first intimation that the hunter has of his presence is the *"bump, bump"* which tells of his departure. Frequently the black-tail will remain perfectly still so as to allow the hunter to pass within a few feet of him, and will then be off like the wind. He also possesses the ability to sneak away from sight through a cover that a stranger would think would not permit of a small dog passing through without being observed, and this too, without making a sound.

· Van Dyke gives the best account of the habits of this deer of any writer that I know of, and there are few sportsmen who will not find some valuable hints in his book in regard to still hunting for game of any description.

THE MOUNTAIN LION.

The mountain lion is a species of panther, something like the Eastern catamount, except larger. It is supposed to be more courageous than the latter, which need not be much, as it is a cowardly brute, except when wounded.

I knew of one near Catamount Pond that was treed by a small dog, and stayed in the tree until the woman of the house took a rifle and went out and shot it. She did not seem to think that she had done anything very wonderful either.

Some years ago they were quite frequent in the neighborhood of the Park, and their mournful screams, like the cry of a lost child, were apt to stampede the grazing animals. In consequence the mountaineers have sought to exterminate them by traps and poison, as well as by shooting, so they are now comparatively scarce. We neither saw or heard any of them during our trip.

WOLVES.

The wolf and the coyote were once extremely numerous in all this section of the country, but they have been nearly exterminated by poisoned carcasses prepared for them by the cattlemen to whom they cause a great loss by killing the young calves. It is said that in consequence of their destruction the prairie dogs are increasing greatly.

A few years since, their howlings were always spoken of by travellers, as one of the ordinary incidents of a camp, as common as that of a cat on a city fence. They have been not only poisoned, but so hunted by cowboys that the few of them that remain keep themselves very secluded. We saw but one coyote, and heard none, nor any wolves during our entire journey.

The latter is the most conclusive proof of their scarcity, as they would gather around a camp in the night and howl, when nothing could be seen of them in the daytime.

BEAVER.

The beaver are very common through the Park, so much so, that at one time the Superintendent allowed them to be killed for fear that if their number was not reduced, they would make so many dams as to flood the narrow valleys and make the Park uninhabitable.

SKUNKS.

Skunks are quite numerous, but there is no proof that their bite has any tendency to hydrophobia, as in the case of those of Kansas and the Indian Territory.

They seem to feed largely on the wild onion, the fumes of which lend an additional sweetness to their scent-giving properties.

They are quite tame or fearless, coming freely around a camp, and not hurrying themselves in the least when disturbed.

OTHER ANIMALS.

The other animals of the Park and its neighborhood are foxes, badgers, rock-dog, an animal somewhat similar to the woodchuck, but smaller, porcupines, the gray hare, the cotton-tail or common rabbit, the jack rabbit and squirrels.

BIRDS.

A large number of eagles are found in the Park and its neighborhood, and a carcass left in any portion of the Park is soon found by the gray bald-head turkey buzzard, or North American vulture, and by the ravens. The buzzard is often seen standing on some arid portion of the prairie, near an alkali pool, apparently rapt in deep meditation. Swans, pelicans and geese are plentiful in all the streams and lakes of the Park, and hatch their young at the mouth of the Upper Yellowstone trail and Pelican Creek. They are also found in great numbers in Henry's Lake and in the streams adjoining it. These waters are also resorted to by vast numbers of ducks.

TURKEY BUZZARD OR NORTH AMERICAN VULTURE.

The cock of the plains, or sage hen, is found in the open portions of the Park and of the surrounding country. Mr. Rosendale told me that he found the great Calmas Meadows, which lie west of Henry's Lake, so full of them that it resembled a barn-yard full of domestic fowl. While there is a prejudice against this bird on the ground that it feeds on sage brush, I confess that our party found it to be very good eating. Whether this is the case in the other months of the year, I am unable to say.

These birds afford admirable sport. They lie well to a dog and get up when approached very much like quail. They fly but a short distance and scatter when they settle, and will then get up one at a time. Later in the season, I understand the shooting is more difficult—that the birds rise together and fly longer, and then settle in such a way that if disturbed a second time they are ready for another flight.

The dusky grouse, blue or "fool" grouse, as it is frequently called from its apparent stupidity, is a mountain bird. It is quite large, a full-grown male weighing about three pounds and a half, and is very delicate eating. They are frequently found alone, walking on the ground. They afford no opportunity for wing shooting, as they will not lie to a dog, and when disturbed fly to a tree. Like an Eastern partridge (ruffled grouse) when treed, they will allow a hunter to fire at them several times before they are disturbed. He should, however, always shoot at the lowest bird.

The willow grouse, otherwise known as the sharp-tail grouse, is found in the thickets of cotton-wood and brush along the streams, and affords great sport to the lovers of wing shooting. It lies well to the dog and its flights are short.

Large numbers of curlew and plover are found upon the prairie, and I understand that they both make their nests upon its surface. I have never hunted them with a dog, but I am informed that neither will lie to one. Sand-hill cranes are frequently found all through this section and are good eating.

Although many game birds are killed by hunters and for shipment East, I imagine that the reduction in the number of wolves and coyotes, which feed upon them and their young, will tend to prevent their decrease.

THE MOUNTAIN GROUSE.

DOGS.

A pointer is probably to be preferred to a setter for a trip of this description, as he can go longer without water. In going through the Park, care should be taken to see that he does not drink any of the bad water which is so often found there, and particularly that he keeps out of the hot springs. An officer from Fort Ellis told me that one of his hunting dogs, a pointer, which he took with him on a trip through the Park, stepped in a little brook which turned out to be hot. The dog immediately looked at his paw with great disgust and went back to his master's tent and never would emerge from it during the rest of the time they remained there. A good dog, on a trip of this kind, would not only be of great assistance in hunting, but would be valuable as a protector of the stock when grazing during the night-time.

The sportsman who visits the Far West, and particularly that portion of it which is occupied for cattle ranges cannot, however, afford to take any valuable dogs with him. The wolf hunters and the cattlemen wage unrelenting war upon all wolves and coyotes, and strychnined carcasses are so strewn over the prairies that it is never certain when a dog will be poisoned.

CHAPTER XXIV.

OUTFIT.

THE RIFLE.—The most important question for the sportsman to consider, is the selection of his rifle ; and there is scarcely any subject on which there is greater difference of opinion than as to what is the best to select. Most American rifles are good, and when one has become so accustomed to a gun of a particular make, and familiar with its mechanism, so that he can operate it with facility, and can humor its weakest points so as to do good shooting, and particularly if he is not thoroughly familiar with the merits of other rifles, he is apt to declare that his own has no superior.

For small game or target work the selection of a rifle is comparatively easy. Any one of the standard varieties can be selected with little of any risk, but my experience and observation leads me to prefer the Remington for this, as for long range practice. The modern tendency, founded upon experience, is towards smaller calibres and higher charges. A few years since most of the rifles used at Creedmoor, Walnut Hill, and other rifle ranges of the country for off-hand work were .44-calibre, using about seventy grains of powder. Now, the best scores on record are being made with .38 and even .32-calibre, and a charge of thirty-five to forty grains of powder. This gives little if any recoil to the rifle and permits a steady holding.

To insure complete accuracy, great attention must be paid to the method of loading. The best short-range shots load their shells at home with precisely the same amount of powder, putting a wad of blotting-paper on top. The bullet is not inserted in the shell, but is pushed into the grooves in the barrel with a stick, so as to be about a thirtieth of an an inch in front of the shell. This causes the bullet to take the grooves perfectly, and prevents the paper patch from being cut by the shoulder of the chamber, giving practically the same result as a muzzle loader. The rifle barrel is carefully cleaned after each shot. Most riflemen use the paper patched bullet, although the naked cannelured ball is preferred by many.

The sights are always the peep and globe. At one time small eye holes in the peep sight were in the majority, but now the best shots are using very large apertures. Some use a hollow bead as a foresight, but I think the ordinary pin is generally preferred. The use of a wind gauge is universal, and a spirit level almost so, although really of very little value in off-hand firing.

These refinements are, of course, entirely unsuited for anything but deliberate target work. While they eliminate all error except such as arises from the personal equation of the rifleman himself, yet the improvement which they give over open-sighted rifles is less than would be supposed to be the case. Many first-class prizes in matches are won to-day by military rifles with open sights, and a six-pound trigger pull, over competitors using rifles having all the above refinements and a three-pound trigger pull.

The great thing in off-handing firing (as in everything else) is practice. This need not necessarily be upon the range. A few minutes a day spent in aiming one's rifle at a spot on the wall and snapping the hammer, will ensure steady holding, and bring the finger and eye to work together as well as if a bullet was fired. I observed that the members of the team of English volunteers that last visited Creedmoor, although veteran shots, were daily in the habit of going to their rooms for aiming practice.

Knowledge of wind and elevations, of course, can only be acquired in the range or in the field.

While many hunters affect to deride "target shooters," in my judgment, it is a mistake to do so. Undoubtedly the experienced hunter will kill more game than a tyro who can beat him at a target. But this is because he knows where the game is likely to be, sees it first, and knows how it will act when alarmed, and consequently is not so taken by surprise as to affect his shooting accurately. But when the other man has learned this, the tables are soon turned. The main drawback to off-hand shooting at rifle ranges, is the tendency it develops to be too slow. Knowing that the target will stay until he gets ready, the rifleman does not fire until he is satisfied with his aim, and consequently is apt to spend too much time in getting it. This sort of man will allow a deer to get out of range before he fires. But this habit can be soon broken by a little practice in rapid aiming. It is important in this that the stock should be of the proper shape so that the sights come into the right position as soon as the rifle is thrown to the face. But practice in aiming is everything. I once had a Ballard, the first rifle I ever owned, which use had made so familiar that when I threw it up so that the stock struck my cheek bone, it was so exactly level that I could, and have done fair shooting, where it was so dark that I could not see the front sight at all. Repeating rifles are almost never used for target firing, as they have a tendency every once and a while to drop a shot. For ordinary shooting, however, they are sufficiently accurate.

But small calibres and light charges are not what is wanted in the Rockies.

For large game, and even for deer, (an animal which possesses an immense vitality) it is necessary that the weapon used should be one which will strike a smashing blow, the shock of which will at once stun and disable the animal, even though not hit in a vital spot. The ordinary sporting rifle does not come up to the standard, even where it has a heavy charge and a forty-four calibre. Its long, pointed and frequently hardened bullet will pass clear through the body of a bear or elk, but although the wound may be mortal the animal will run a long way before it succumbs. Such a rifle is therefore inferior to one which throws a ball which opens on striking so that the whole force of its velocity is expended in its impact, the difference being that which exists between the thrust of a stiletto and a blow with a sledge-hammer.

I have previously * described how this result was obtained by the Winchester I carried, which was forty-five calibre, using seventy-five grains of powder and a Keene bullet weighing three hundred and fifty grains. The defect of this gun is one that is common to all rifles using that charge of powder with such a heavy bullet, *i. e.*, its high trajectory. If sighted for a point blank of 150 yards, it would carry over 2.59 inches at 25 yards, 4.91 at 50 yards, 5.66 at 75 yards, 5.17 at 100 yards, 3.41 at 125 yards, and would fall below 5.05 inches at 175 yards, and 11.19 inches at 200 yards, while a bullet of 270 grains with a charge of 113 grains, had so much greater velocity that it only rose .96 inches at 25 yards, 2.16 at 50, 2.72 at 75, 2.73 at 100, and 1.73 at 125, and fell 2.52 at 175 yards at 6.09 at 200 ; the difference between the two guns, being that the latter is never three inches out of the direct line, while the former is always from two and a half to over six inches. On the other hand the light bullet soon looses its momentum, so that the heavier one has a much longer accurate range.

The question of range, however, is not so important as that of a flat trajectory. Most game is shot within 200 yards. Beyond that distance the difficulty of accu-

* See page 40.

rately estimating the distance makes shooting a good deal
of a lottery. Even within 200 yards it is very hard in
varying conditions of light, in the woods and over broken
ground, to guess the distance within thirty yards. I
know of an army officer who was a good target shot, insist on elevating his sight to 200 yards to fire at a deer that
was not 60 yards from him, because he saw him through
a vista in the woods, which magnified the distance. It is
therefore a good rule to always shoot low, and to under
estimate distances.

The difficulty of controlling the elevations of the Winchester I have found to be so solved by the use of the
Freund sight, that personally, I have no desire to change
my rifle.

At the same time it is certain that a rifle with a strong
breech mechanism, such as the Sharp or Hepburn, loaded
on the Express system with from 100 to 110 grains of
powder, and a bullet of about 275 grains, the latter having
a small hole bored through into its apex, is as powerful
and deadly weapon as can be used. Almost the only
factory cartridge which comes near this standard is the
40-90-370 Sharp's. The Winchester Express is fairly
good, but has more lead in proportion to the powder.
The heavy charge and light bullet of these rifles gives
such velocity that no alteration need be made in the sights
in shooting up to 200 yards, and a deer or antelope would
be certain to be hit anywhere within that distance. On
striking, the bullet flies to pieces, giving a terrific concus-
sion and tearing the vitals of the animal struck, into
fragments.

Mr. T. S. Van Dyke (who I consider to be the best
authority on this subject, and whose book, the "Still
Hunter," should be in the hands of every hunter), carries
a double-barreled .50-calibre rifle built on this method,
but carrying a heavier ball, on the theory that he would
rather "tote" a fourteen-pound gun which drops any-

thing it is fired at, than chase a crippled deer all the afternoon. His judgment is, and I concur in it, that the Express bullet must be heavy enough to give plenty of penetration, as too light a bullet, or one with too large a hole in front, so that it breaks up into many pieces, while deadly in the extreme if it strikes in a soft place, does not do much harm if it hits where great penetration is required. For this reason, if it was not for the question of elevation, I would recommend the Keene bullet in preference to the Express. Heavy charges involve a correspondingly heavy recoil. This can be largely obviated by a rubber butt plate, and otherwise must be put up with as inevitable. If the right elbow is thrown well up, and the rifle butt held with the right hand hard against the shoulder instead of the muscles of the arm, a heavy charge can be fired without injury.

The question of whether the single loader with its Express charge is not superior to the repeater, is one as to which there is a great difference of opinion. Some riflemen, who I consider to be the most qualified by experience and judgment to express an opinion, insist that it is, and that they can load it so fast as to equalize the advantages of a repeater in that respect. For myself, I can only say that I use a 45.75 Winchester, and so long as I can buy Keene bullets, am satisfied with it for hunting purposes. There is a great controversy as to how it compares with the Bullard, as to which I express no opinion, never having used the latter. Its action is certainly more silent than that of the Winchester.

I do not think very much of explosive bullets. If they strike the head or neck they are very fatal. But they lack penetration and are little if any better in a side shot than a solid ball. I know a gentleman who struck an antelope with several; four, I think, without killing him. He could see every bullet explode as it struck, but none of them accomplished anything beyond making a bad flesh wound.

It must not be understood that I favor such an arrangement of the sights as makes the point blank on the Winchester a hundred and fifty yards. I simply mentioned this as an illustration, being founded upon tests by a correspondent of the " American Field," in whose accuracy I have great faith. In my own opinion, this arrangement of the sights is objectionable, as involving altogether too much over shooting at intermediate distances. I should consider a point blank of a hundred yards to be about correct. And this should be with the front sight drawn so as to be distinctly visible. On my own rifle I take in the whole head of the pin to give the point blank for this distance. This gives but a slight rise in shooting at the intermediate distances, and even then, for a close shot, as in firing at the head of a grouse at fifty feet, the aim must be very fine, a thing which requires cool nerves and a steady hand. Van Dyke considers that the point blank sight should be so set as not to give a rise at the highest intermediate point exceeding one inch for the woods, two and a half inches for open, hilly ground, and four inches for the plains. The sportsman must also be careful to aim low at the midway point, and in firing down hill, in dim light, or against the sun.

I am firmly of opinion that the present method of sighting our military rifles is a blunder. With practically all of them, the aim in firing at a hundred yards must be at least a foot under the mark, and that, too, with the front sight drawn as fine as possible. If a soldier in action uses a coarse sight, this would more than double the distance his piece would carry over. Yet at a hundred yards is just the time and place where the aim must be exact. This method of sighting explains how the British soldiers were shot down like rabbits by the Boers in South Africa, and how the Zulus and Arabs could charge up to the bayonets of a line of men armed with breech-loaders without being exterminated. The British shot too high, and the nearer their assailants got the safer they were.

The sights which are placed upon a hunting rifle are a matter of the greatest importance, and yet is one that is generally neglected. The average sportsman buys his rifle as it is turned out of the factory, and without question as to the character of the sights, and the manufacturer is apt to follow the cheapest and most antiquated pattern as long as it sells. Consequently the average rifle sight is wretched.

When the standard pattern is departed from, the field for individual choice becomes large, for there are few subjects upon which more hobbies exist. Eye-sight, the country in which the shooting is done and more than all habit, come in to warp the judgment.

Good hunting sights must show plainly in all lights, be such as can be quickly caught and should afford a large field of vision. A rear sight with high sides, like many "buck horn" sights, is objectionable as cutting off a view of the game. Too fine a notch, or the use of a fine sight is incompatible with rapid shooting. In fact I am an advocate for the use of a full sight even in target shooting. Van Dyke uses a straight bar, trusting to his eye to catch the centre, and is careful to stain his sights so as to avoid all reflection. The important thing in all hunting is elevation. Killing shots must be delivered within a small space. An eight-inch circle will take in the fore-shoulder, heart and lungs of a deer, which constitutes his vitals. If a variation outside this is made it should be in a horizontal and not a perpendicular direction. The former will hit the animal somewhere, but the latter will be a clean miss. The bead shape of the head of the Freund sight is one of its strong points, as it enables the person using it to know exactly how he is holding. It is much easier to talk about full and half sights than it is to actually adjust them with the ordinary sights in practice, particularly when one is in a hurry. If the front sight is brass or bright metal, the reflection of the sun upon it gives it a false centre (if it does not dazzle the eye so that it cannot be seen clearly) and makes one shoot towards the sun and too high. If black, it is difficult to see it in the woods or in a dim light. A dark sight with a piece of platina or ivory in-laid in its lower edge is the best.

The " Beach " sight is very good for target shooting, but I never was able to see the pin clearly enough to use it in the woods. Perhaps if the pin were gilt it would show better. But even then, the gilt would not be likely to show, as the hood would keep off the rays of light so as to prevent their being reflected.

GENERAL OUTFIT.

The following is a list of articles required on a trip of this description. Those in italics being all that will be required if the trip is made in stages.

FOR GENTLEMEN—CLOTHING.—*Coat,* drab Norfolk jacket is preferable ; next, an old, comfortable business coat. *Vest and trousers,* used the preceding winter ; gray or drab colored. If the trip is to be made on horse-back, the trousers should be strong and sound in the seat. It is also advisable to have a pair of canvas trou-sers to use as overalls or for a change. *Hat,* sun hel-met, or wide-brimmed, drab felt (both had better be taken). *Knit cap,* to sleep in.

Shoes, stout and comfortable. If style is no object, the Yerrington & Quinby waterproof hunting shoe, with water tight tongue and hob nails is the best for climbing and fishing. The single sole is preferable to the double sole, being lighter. For the same reason I prefer the shoe to the boot. *Light shoes,* for change ; canvas shoes with rubber sole for still hunting. Moccasins are good, but your feet have to become toughened before you can use them with comfort. *Slippers, rubbers;* if ordinary shoes are worn, the latter are necessary.

Cardigan jacket, thick overcoat. I found that with a thick coat and Cardigan jacket, my overcoat was unnecessary. It would be otherwise, however, in riding in a wagon when the sun was not up. *Two thick lawn tennis overshirts* (drab for hunters); *two suits medium underclothes; one suit extra heavy underclothes* for cold nights; *six pairs medium socks;* two pairs heavy, long stockings; one pair heavy, short stockings (to sleep in); *silk neck handkerchief; six silk pocket handkerchiefs; thin rubber coat; pair thick buckskin gloves,* coming high on the wrist; *pair old kid gloves;* canvas shooting jacket; canvas leggings, with Napoleon tops (to keep the knee dry when kneeling), and side straps, well put on. Those with cord and catches on are apt to get out of order.

Canteen; *large pocket knife,* one with corkscrew, screw driver, etc.; *field glass,* a small opera glass is much more convenient, and if first-class, will answer all purposes; *watch,* cheap stem winder; pocket drinking cup of folding leather; *goggles,* smoke colored; *match safe,* flint and steel, compass, these three should never be parted from by the sportsman.

Note book, letter paper, stamped envelopes, pencils and stylographic pen, postal cards.

Cotton batting, to pack anything fragile on the return. *Toilet articles,* carried in a roll-up dressing case; *soap* (carbolic), in tin box; *three towels; flesh gloves or brush; hair brush; sponge, in oil silk bag; comb; tooth brush and powder; razor,* etc. (for those who shave); *small hand glass; toilet paper; court plaster; roll of surgeon's plaster; box cuticura; whisk broom; pocket flask; pack of cards; traveling lamp; large rubber bands; box zinc ointment, box glycerate of starch* for sunburn; the latter to be used in the morning, the former at night.

LADIES' CLOTHING.—*Dress*, heavy flannel, drab, to come to top of walking boots; *extra flannel skirt;* trousers to match dress, cut Turkish fashion; *underwear, flannels*, same as gentleman's, *dozen muslin drawers.* If the journey is to be on horseback, the under drawers should be fulled below the knees. One pair extra heavy flannels for night, to be worn over the day flannels; *Cardigan jacket*; *heavy ulster*, Jersey preferable; *gossamer waterproof; hat and long gloves*, same as gentlemen; vail, wide and three yards long.

Shoes, high, heavy walking boots of oil-dressed leather, and low shoes for a change; *rubber over-shoes* to cover the instep.

Blanket shawls; silk net for the hair; roll up dressing case; umbrella, small.

"Red Riding-Hood" with cape, coming below the elbows, of flannel, to sleep in; *two pairs thick, woolen stockings; six pairs cotton stockings; two dozen linen handkerchiefs; two silk neck-handkerchiefs.*

MISCELLANEOUS.

Tobacco; two pipes; thread and needles; scissors; buttons; thimble; house-wife for sewing materials; pieces of cloth for patches; *Nux vomica, or Seidlitz powders; Seltzsers aperient; fly medicine; guide book; map;* bag of odds and ends; rivets; shoe-maker's wax; winding silk; fine copper wire, etc.

Tools.—My box is three by six by one and a half inches, and contains thirty tools of good steel fitting into a single handle and is simply invaluable.

Ball of twine; shoe strings; shoe-maker's thread.

SPORTING OUTFIT.—Rifle and case; 200 cartridges; twelve bore and case; 200 cartridges, loaded with 6. 4. and buck; four boxes Schluber's thread-wound cartridges; auxiliary rifle barrel; two boxes cartridges for same ; revolver and cartridges ; oiler and rags ; wiping-stick and brush ; two cartridge belts ; canvas bag for cartridges ; rods ; reels ; fly books ; landing net ; flies, mostly dark or yellow coachmen ; two lines ; six leaders ; twelve hooks ; spring scales ; box of small rubber bands (to slip around line in going through brush) ; canvas fish basket, folding ; wading drawers, to come up to the waist.

Bedding for each person, mattress, thin and flexible ; rubber blanket ; four blankets ; buffalo robe ; pillow and two cases ; mosquito netting ; canvas, one large square for a floor cloth, and to roll up the bedding of the party ; straps for roll of bedding.

Camp outfit for a party.—Wall tent ; poles and pins (a canvas partition to suspend from the ridge pole is a great convenience) ; camp chairs, folding (and always breaking) ; valise for each person ; candlesticks ; two wash basins ; two water pails and cups ; camp table, folding ; ten plates ; ten cups ; six knives and forks ; twelve spoons (six table, six tea) ; one gallon coffee pot ; one camp kettle ; one half gallon coffee pot ; one dish pan ; one coffee mill ; two pudding pans ; paper tinned tacks, large size ; two frying pans with long handles ; axe ; shovel ; Dutch oven (cast-iron) ; gridiron ; corkscrew ; one candle lantern without springs ; one pound assorted nails ; sixty feet copper wire ; six bags, unbleached muslin, to strain the coffee.

Supplies for seven people for four weeks.—Twenty-nine pounds ham, sixty pounds bacon, one hundred pounds flour, fifty pounds potatoes, twenty-four pounds sugar, twelve pounds coffee, four pounds yeast powder, ten pounds salt, five pounds Alden dried apples, three pounds candles, two pounds Durham tobacco, fifteen pounds butter, quarter pound of tea, six pounds cheese, one pound pepper, four pounds prunes, six dozen eggs, twelve cans tomatoes, twelve cans corn, twelve cans peaches, twelve cans sardines, two cans blackberry jam, fourteen cans condensed milk, three cans tongue, six cans corned beef, sixteen boxes matches, four bottles chow chow, one gallon maple syrup, two cases beer, six quarts whiskey.

Horse equipment.—Saddles, particularly the side-saddles, to be examined carefully before starting to see if in good order, and that they do not chafe the horses backs; saddle blankets; bridles; riding whips (better than spurs); picket ropes; hobbles.

CHAPTER XXV.

FLORA OF THE PARK.

Nearly eighty per cent of the Park is covered with dense forests, mainly of the black or bastard fir, black spruce, white pine, red and balsam fir. Considerable ancient timber is now found fossilized upon the mountain slopes, which is evidently much larger and mainly of different varieties from that now found in the Park, probably embracing a smaller proportion of the coniferæ.

Black or bastard fir is far the largest variety of timber now growing in the Park, and is usually found scattered through forests of smaller timber near the Mammoth Hot Springs, Tower Falls, Upper Yellowstone, and other elevated terraces. It is often found from three to five feet in diameter and 150 feet in height, and is not unlike the Eastern hemlock in the irregular form of its branched-top as well as the coarse-grained, shaky, and inferior quality of its timber. Usually it is much smaller and is even more worthless for shade than it is lumber.

Black spruce, growing on the moist, sheltered slopes of the mountains, near the snow, though having a smaller trunk, is fully as tall as the black fir, and is a statelier tree and more valuable for lumber.

Red fir is the next in size (which nearly equals that of the Norway pine of Michigan) and the first in value of any tree in the Park for hewn-timber for building bridges, etc., for which purposes it is admirably adapted. It is abundant in all except the very elevated regions.

White pine, rivaling in symmetrical beauty the white pine of the East, but much inferior in size, and somewhat in quality, is the prevailing timber of most of the elevated terrace groves, and occasionally of the narrow valleys and cañon passes of the mountains. It grows very densely, often rendering traveling among it upon horseback exceedingly difficult when standing, and utterly impossible when burned and fallen, as it is over large areas of the Park, where it proves one of the greatest impediments to exploring as well as to improvement by roads and bridle-paths. It is the best material found in the Park for lumber, shingles, small timber, rafters, fence-poles, etc.

Balsam fir, somewhat different from that of the Alleghanies, is abundant and very beautiful, singly or in dense groves or isolated clumps scattered over the grassy slopes, just below the mountain snow-fields.

Cedar of a red or spotted variety, growing low and very branched, but with timber valuable for fence-posts, is abundant.

Poplar or aspen is found in dense thickets among the sheltered foot-hills. Dwarf maple, with leaves often scarlet with fungus, is sparingly found, and innumerable dense thickets of willow; the main value of all these last named varieties being for the food of game in the winter and of the beaver in all season. The thickets of willow are the resort of the cow-elks in the breeding season, and they hide in it with their calves until they are large enough to venture out into the open country with safety.

It is very much to be regretted that through the carelessness of camping parties, immense tracts of woodland have been burned over. As a consequence it is not uncommon, in going through the Park, to be compelled to pass by mile after mile of charred and blackened tree trunks, instead of riding in the refreshing shade of the woods. This mainly if not entirely results from a want of the simplest precaution with respect to camp fires. This wanton destruction of the forests should be checked by the severe punishment of the offenders, and the efforts of the Superintendent to stop it should be aided by Congressional legislation.

In addition to the forest growths, there are many kinds of shrubs, flowers and grasses. The choke cherry, the goose-berry, the buffalo-berry, the bull-berry, and black and red currants are found along the streams and in moist places of the middle and lower altitudes. The meadows and hill-sides are spangled with bright colored flowers, among which may be noted the bee-larkspur, the columbine, the harebell, the lupin, the evening primrose, the aster, the painted cup, the gentian and various kinds of euphorbia. It is not uncommon to find daisies, buttercups, forget-me-nots, white ground phlox and other field flowers flourishing in profusion near the melting snow banks during the month of August. Scarcely a night throughout the year passes without frost, even though the temperature by day is over 80°F., so that all forms of vegetation in the Park grow and bloom under somewhat unusual conditions. Indeed, when ice forms in the water pails of camping parties during the night, as often happens, and the petals of the flowers become crisp with frost, even then the blooms are not harmed, but thaw out bright and fresh when the hot sun touches them. The pasturage on the many open spaces is excellent, the mountain meadows being covered with a mat of nutritious grasses. The predominating variety is the bunch grass, upon which the horses of tourists generally subsist, keeping in good condition without the need of oats. Among other kinds are the blue-joint, fescue and beard grasses, as well as Alpine timothy, all of which grow luxuriantly.

CHAPTER XXVI.

ALTITUDES OF THE PARK.

The following are the altitudes of the principal points within the Park as given in report of the United States Geological Survey :

	FEET.
Amethyst Mountain	9,423
Bunsen's Peak	8,775
Cascade Creek, at camping ground	7,912
Crater Hills or Sulphur Mountain	7,820
Divide between Yellowstone and Madison Rivers	8,164
Dunraven Peak	9,988
Gardner River, mouth of	5,300
Gibbon River, head of cañon	7,350
Lower Geyser Basin	7,252
Madison Lake	8,300
Madison River, at foot of second cañon	6,605
Mammoth Hot Springs :	
At Hotel	6,387
Summit above on Norris Road	7,310
Mary's Lake	8,336
Mount Doane	10,713
Mount Evarts	7,600
Mount Langford	10,799
Mount Stevenson	10,420
Mount Washburn	10,346
Mud Geysers on Yellowstone River	7,712
Norris Geyser Basin	7,527
Quadrant Mountain	10,127
Shoshone Geyser Basin	7,881
Shoshone Lake	7,830
Upper Geyser Basin, near Old Faithful	7,372
Yellowstone Lake	7,738

FEET.

Yellowstone River :

	FEET.
At Mud Geysers	7,705
Upper Fall, top	7,693
Upper Fall, bottom	7,581
Lower Fall, top	7,575
Lower Fall, bottom	7,275
Mouth Tower Creek	6,207
Mouth East Fork	5,970
Yellowstone Cañon, east side, top of, at falls	7,710

For purposes of comparison the following heights are given.

FEET.

	FEET.
Mount Washington, White Mountains	6,428
" Marcy, Adirondacks	5,379
" Mansfield, Vermont	4,430
Ben Nevis, highest in Great Britain	4,406
Vesuvius, Italy	3,948
Round Top, Catskills	3,804

Notwithstanding these great altitudes, the cold does not seem to be nearly so severe in the Park as would be the case in the East at anything like the same height.

According to the reports of the Superintendent the mean temperature during several years was :

IN JULY AND AUGUST.		IN SEPTEMBER.	
Sunrise	50° to 50°	Sunrise	36° to 41°
Mid-day	68° to 80°	Mid-day	60° to 66°
Sunset	62° to 69°	Sunset	50° to 58°
Mean	60° to 67°	Mean	46° to 55°

The snow lies a long time, but the cold is not severe, even in the depths of winter.

CHAPTER XXVII.

DISTANCES AND TIME TABLE FOR A TOUR THROUGH THE PARK.

	Miles.	Time.
St. Paul to Livingston (rail)	1032	45 hours.
Livingston to Cinnabar (rail)	51	3 "
Cinnabar to Mammoth Springs (stage)	6	1 "
Total	1089	49 hours.

Spend one day at Mammoth Springs. If time permits, spend another visiting the falls of the Gardner, particularly the Middle Falls.

MAMMOTH SPRINGS TO FORKS OF THE FIREHOLE (BY STAGE).
(THIRD DAY.)

	Miles.	Total Miles.
From Mammoth Hot Springs to Terrace Pass	—	1.93
Swan Lake	3.21	5.14
Crossing of Middle Fork of Gardner River	2.33	7.47
Willow Park, upper end	3.50	10.97
Obsidan Cliffs and Beaver Lake	1.37	12.34
Green Creek	1.40	13.74
Lake of the Woods	.76	14.50
Hot Springs	1.68	16.18
Norris Fork Crossing	4.17	20.35
Norris Geyser Basin	.71	21.06

Dine, and spend two hours examining the geysers and mud pots.

	Miles	Miles.
Geyser Creek and Forks of the Paint	3.13	24.19
Head of Gibbon Cañon and foot bridge on trail to Monument Geysers	.72	24.91
Falls of the Gibbon River	3.75	28.66
Cañon Creek	.59	29.25
Earthquake Cliffs	3.00	32.25
Lookout Terrace	1.50	33.75
Hotel at Forks of the Firehole River	2.43	36.18

This road is good, and the distance from the Mammoth Springs can be covered in one day.

(FOURTH DAY.)

	Miles.	Miles.
Hotel to Forks of road at Prospect Point	—	1.00
Old Camp Reunion	1.00	2.00
Fountain Geyser, in the Lower Geyser Basin	1.00	3.00
Excelsior Geyser, in Midway Geyser Basin	2.00	5.00
Old Faithful, in Upper Geyser Basin	6.00	11.00

The stage arrives at the geysers in the forenoon. That day and the next (fifth) should be spent here.

If it is intended to visit the Yellowstone Lake, it will be wise to leave the Upper Geysers and take the trail along the west side of Yellowstone Lake to the Great Cañon. This must now be made on horseback, and will take a day and a half. The night must be spent at the Lake. (This trip will occupy the sixth and seventh days).

	Miles.	Miles.
Old Faithful to Kepler's Cascades	—	1.94
Leech Lake	2.72	4.66
Norris Pass, Continental Divide	3.00	7.66
De Lacey Creek, Pacific waters	.97	8.63
Two Ocean Pond, on Continental Divide	3.50	12.13
Hot Spring, at head of Thumb, on Yellowstone Lake	2.99	15.12
Hot Spring, on Lake shore	2.02	17.14
Hot Spring Creek	4.00	21.14
Natural Bridge	7.44	28.58
Fort of Yellowstone Lake (bridle path)	4.68	33.26
Grizzly Creek	3.26	36.52
Giant's Cauldron and Belching Spring	3.00	39.52
Forks of road from the Forks of the Firehole to the Cañon	2.00	41.52

The following is the usual stage route from the geysers (sixth day.)

UPPER GEYSERS OF THE GREAT CAÑON.

	Miles.	Miles.
Upper Geysers to Forks of the Firehole	—	11.00
Forks of the road near Prospect Point	1	12.00
Hot Springs	1.08	13.08
Rock Ford	3.86	16.94
Willow Creek	2.00	18.94
Fort of the Grade up the Madison Divide	2.00	20.94
Upper end of Mary's Lake	1.91	22.85
Sulphur Lake and Hot Springs	1.12	23.97
Alum Creek Camp	2.00	25.97
Sage Creek	2.00	27.97
Fork of the road to Yellowstone Lake, *	5.00	32.97

	Miles.	Miles.
Sulphur Mountain	1.50	34.47
Alum Creek	1.61	36.08
Upper Falls of the Yellowstone	3.26	39.34
Crystal Falls and Grotto Pool	.40	39.74
Great Falls of the Yellowstone	.24	39.98

This is driven over in one day, but is a pretty fatiguing drive, as the road up the Divide is not good.

Remain at the Cañon one day, (the seventh, if the Lake has been visited, the eighth). If Mount Washburn is not visited, the return will be to the Forks of the Firehole, and thence to the Mammoth Springs, (on the eighth day or, if the Lake has been visited, the ninth.)

The following route should be substituted, whenever possible, it must however, be made on horseback. It will occupy a day (the eighth, or, if the Lake has been visited, the ninth.)

MOUNT WASHBURN BRIDLE-PATH.

	Miles.	Miles.
Grand Cañon to Cascade Creek	—	2.00
Summit of Mount Washburn	7.22	9.22
Forks of trail	4.13	13.35
Tower Falls	1.87	15.22

(* Here those intending to visit the Lake turn off, and after visiting it, return to this road and continue over it to the cañon).

There is a good wagon road from Yancy's at Tower Falls, and those who do not care to ride on horseback to the Mammoth Springs, can have a stage meet them at the former, the Falls.

TOWER FALLS TO THE MAMMOTH SPRINGS.

	Miles.	Miles.
Tower Falls to Forks of the Yellowstone (Baronette Bridge)	—	3.19
Pleasant Valley	2.48	5.67
Dry Cañon or Devil's Cut	2.28	7.95
Lava beds	4.69	12.64
Black-tail Deer Creek	2.00	14.64
Upper Falls, East Fork of Gardner River	2.70	17.34
Bridge over " " " " "	2.06	19.40
Bride over Gardner River	.38	.78
Mammoth Springs	1.77	21.55

This will require but half a day—the ninth, or if the Lake has been visited, the tenth.

If the trip must be curtailed, it should be in the following order : First, the trip to the Yellowstone Lake ; second, Mount Washburn ; third, Middle Falls of the Gardner ; fourth, one day at the Upper Geysers ; fifth, one day at Mammoth Springs. It is poor policy, however, to omit thoroughly seeing any of the wonders of the Park to save a day or two.

IDAHO YESTERDAYS SERIES

JUDITH AUSTIN, IDAHO STATE HISTORICAL SOCIETY

GENERAL EDITOR

The Idaho Yesterdays Series is a series of classic Idaho and regional books, in reprint editions, developed by the Idaho State Historical Society. This series makes important out-of-print publications on Idaho and its history available to a wide audience. Scholarly introductions and supplementary materials enhance access to and the usefulness of these fascinating literary and historical milestones in the culture of the early West.

OTHER IDAHO YESTERDAYS TITLES

The Bannock of Idaho
by Brigham D. Madsen

✧

Journal of an Exploring Tour Beyond the Rocky Mountains
by Samuel Parker
Introduction by
Larry R. Jones

✧

The Nez Perces Since Lewis & Clark
by Kate McBeth
Introduction by Peter Iverson
and Elizabeth James

✧

Stump Ranch Pioneer
by Nelle Portrey Davis
Introduction by
Susan Hendricks Swetnam

The Resources and Attractions of Idaho Territory
by Robert E. Strahorn
Introduction by Judith Austin

✧

Silver Strike:
The True Story of Silver Mining in the Coeur d'Alenes
by William T. Stoll
Introduction by
Katherine G. Aiken

✧

A Ram in the Thicket:
The Story of a Roaming Homesteader Family on the Mormon Frontier
by Frank C. Robertson
Introduction by
Charles S. Peterson
Afterword by
Glen E. Robertson

UNIVERSITY OF IDAHO PRESS
16 BRINK HALL· MOSCOW IDAHO 83844-1107
800-847-7377

MAP OF THE YELLOWSTONE NATIONAL PARK
Compiled from different official explorations and our personal survey, 1882.
CARL J. HAAS and A. RYDSTRÖM, Civil Engineers.

MAP OF THE
YELLOWSTONE NATIONAL PARK
AND SURROUNDING COUNTRY.